MULTICULTURALISM IN THE COLLEGE CURRICULUM

MULTICULTURALISM IN THE COLLEGE CURRICULUM

A Handbook of Strategies and Resources for Faculty

Marilyn Lutzker

The Greenwood Educators' Reference Collection

GREENWOOD PRESS
Westport, Connecticut • London

Library of Congress Cataloging-in-Publication Data

Lutzker, Marilyn.
   Multiculturalism in the college curriculum : a handbook of
strategies and resources for faculty / Marilyn Lutzker.
       p.   cm. — (The Greenwood educators' reference collection,
ISBN 1056–2192)
   Includes bibliographical references (p.   ) and index.
   ISBN 0–313–28918–2 (alk. paper)
   1. Universities and colleges—United States—Curricula.
   2. Multiculturalism—Study and teaching (Higher)—United States.
   3. Pluralism (Social sciences)—Study and teaching (Higher)—United
States. I. Title. II. Series.
LB2361.5.L88   1995
378.1′99′0973—dc20   94–37880

British Library Cataloguing in Publication Data is available.

Library of Congress Catalog Card Number: 94–37880
ISBN: 0–313–28918–2
ISSN: 1056–2192

First published in 1995

Greenwood Press, 88 Post Road West, Westport, CT 06881
An imprint of Greenwood Publishing Group, Inc.

Printed in the United States of America

∞™

The paper used in this book complies with the
Permanent Paper Standard issued by the National
Information Standards Organization (Z39.48–1984).

10 9 8 7 6 5 4 3 2 1

Contents

Preface

My hope is that ultimately academia (and the rest of the world) will become so accustomed to multiculturalism in the curriculum that we will no longer notice it, discuss it, or need to applaud its inclusion.

In the meantime, this book has been written for instructors in all disciplines who believe that diversity in the curriculum is an important goal for higher education today but who, for various reasons, have not yet made such revisions in their syllabi. The book is not addressed to those individuals and institutions who are undertaking full-scale curriculum revision projects. Accordingly, the reader will find in the pages that follow a practical handbook for making small additions and changes in individual syllabi and not a blueprint for large-scale restructuring. The underlying belief is that even small changes can be effective and that a multitude of such small changes across an entire syllabus or college curriculum can make a significant difference.

Among the advantages and delights of being a librarian is the experience of being a generalist accustomed to browsing the literature of many disciplines; thus although there is much in this book which is original, there is more which has been gleaned from the literature of higher education and of the multitude of disciplines included within it. I have read many books and articles and spoken to many people in the course of this research. I have attempted to give credit where it was due, but one can't always be sure where an idea really came from. Accordingly, I would like to thank not only the people I have cited in notes and the bibliography, but also the many whose contributions may be unacknowledged.

I have had much support and help in researching and writing this book. My sincere thanks are due to my colleagues at John Jay College of Criminal Justice, especially those with whom I am privileged to work in the library. It is a pleasure to also offer special thanks to the John Jay College Faculty Senate for allowing me to present a preliminary draft of this book at a Better Teaching Seminar, and to the City University of New York Research Foundation for providing a small grant to cover expenses. Finally, a grateful acknowledgment to those friends who so kindly provided critical readings of the manuscript at key points: Wanda Evans, Eli Faber, Olive James, Karen Kaplowitz, Robert J. Lowenherz, and Zoe Salem.

Introduction

This book is a practical guide for teaching faculty in all disciplines who believe that multiculturalism/diversity in the college curriculum is a worthwhile goal. No attempt will be made to argue the validity of such a goal; belief in it is an underlying assumption of the book.

There has been much discussion—and no agreement—over the meanings of multiculturalism and diversity, and the extent to which they mean the same thing. I will use the words interchangeably to describe a broad instructional approach to every discipline in which students will be provided with the opportunity to think about those who might be different from themselves in race, ethnicity, religion, gender, age, and class. I also believe it is essential to place this thinking within a global context. Students in this country must understand that we are all "the other" to the rest of the world.

Diversity is about expanding horizons. One need only look at a college curriculum of one hundred years ago to see that revising today's curriculum is part of a long and continuous process. Well-meaning people at that time opposed the adding of modern history to the curriculum because it would take time away from the study of the biblical and classical eras. They were also adamant in their belief that there was no place in the curriculum for science. Later, after the acceptance of physics and chemistry into the curriculum, it was argued with equal vehemence that psychology and sociology were too unscientific to be considered academic disciplines. (And then, there was the issue of higher education for women. . .)

Curricular changes have always been difficult and accompanied by anguished cries from both sides because they require a basic redefinition of what is worthy of study. Although it is easy today to laugh at arguments against the study of psychology or French (or the concept of higher education for women), one must recognize that arguments about the academic legitimacy of courses in the psychology of women or Kiswahili are still entertained.

Scholars today are finding it necessary to redefine their disciplines and to shift the nature of scholarly inquiry. As Lawrence W. Levine said in his presidential address to the Organization of American Historians, "The colloquy is no longer focused primarily on interpretations of discrete events, it has increasingly shifted ground to a concern over matters of legitimacy: *Which* events, *which* individuals, *which* groups are worth having a colloquy about in the first place?"[1] He also notes how "seductive and perilous is the trap of the assumed truth. Certain ideas become so deeply ingrained, so taken for granted, that they do not seem like ideas at all but part of the natural order."[2]

It is widely assumed that certain subjects, like history, sociology, and literature, are good candidates for incorporating diversity, while others, like science, mathematics, and economics, are not. Given the broad definition of diversity—to include gender, class (hence, power or the lack of it), and the world beyond the United States and Western Europe, as well as race and ethnicity—this assumption is not necessarily true. Thus, readers will find that throughout this book attention has been paid to the "less likely candidates" among the subjects.

MODELS OF CURRICULUM DIVERSITY

There are many ways to introduce diversity into the curriculum. Theorists from African American studies and from women studies have provided us with useful descriptions of stages of what is now generally called curriculum revision. These stages can be viewed historically and as a continuum.

1. Exclusion: The curriculum is based on the accomplishments and thinking of traditional white, male, Euro-Americans from the middle and upper classes. Minorities, other parts of the world, women, and the working class (except in rebellion) are largely ignored.

2. Little boxes: The accomplishments of superstar minority and female figures are added to a course in politics and government, or a half-hour lecture on all of Asia is added to a world history course, without basically changing the outlook of what is being presented for the semester.

3. Specialized studies: Courses are developed which are directed to issues of minorities and women and which attempt to see the world from this new perspective. These courses, whether offered in separate departments or incorporated into traditional disciplines, reach only a very small percentage of students who are already interested in the subject.

4. Diversity requirements: Increasingly, colleges are requiring that all students take at least one course to satisfy a "diversity requirement." Whether chosen from a menu of courses offered by several departments or from specially designed courses, this approach ensures that some of the issues related to diversity will be brought to all of the students. It does, however, still keep issues of mulitculturalism isolated from the mainstream.

5. A transformed curriculum: Consideration is given to the perspectives and experiences of the entire world and all groups within it.[3]

Many educators adhere to the concept that a total rewriting of every course syllabus is the *only* true road to diversity. As noted in the preface, this book is predicated on the belief that there is a middle way between the traditional approaches and a complete overhaul of the curriculum.

The types of strategies discussed in the following chapters are clearly not the only way to broaden the curriculum. They are one way, however, and a practical one for those who are hesitant about undertaking larger-scale revisions. *The content of the course need not be weakened or made less academically stringent by adopting any of the suggestions offered.*

FREQUENTLY CITED REASONS FOR NOT INCLUDING DIVERSITY

Instructors who believe in the concept of a multicultural curriculum but have not yet undertaken any changes in their own approach often give one or more of the following reasons for their hesitation:

1. "Since I don't belong to a minority group, there will be resentment if I try to teach about one."

2. "I don't know anything about the subject, and I have enough trouble keeping up with the literature of my own field."

3. "Students already have a wide range of ethnic studies and women studies courses they can take. They are better off learning the material from specialists."

4. "There is no room in my syllabus." (This is the most common reason and the one which seems most incontrovertible.)

The purpose of this book is to provide practical answers to such dilemmas. Following are some preliminary comments on these issues.

"I can't teach about minority or oppressed groups because I have not experienced their problems, and those in the class who have will resent my attempts."

Although we unashamedly teach about the Aztecs, the Egyptians, and the crusaders, politics both on campus and in the larger world have raised this issue—baldly stated as "if you haven't lived it, you can't teach it"—to the point where in many places it must be argued and refuted. Henry Louis Gates, an African American who is one of the most respected scholars in the field of African American studies, has written: "African-American studies is not just for Blacks; our subject is open to all—to study or to teach. The fundamental premise of the academy is that all things ultimately are knowable; all are therefore teachable."[4] Most of us experience a special feeling when teaching about "our" group, be it religious, ethnic, professional, or geographic. I may feel an imperative when teaching about Jews from Poland who settled in New York, but that does not mean I cannot be as effective teaching about the popes of Renaissance Italy. Although it is true that one who is not a member of a particular group can not know what it feels like to be such, it is also true that one can, from the outside, teach about those on the inside, and call on the insiders (personally and through their writings) to speak for themselves.[5]

"I don't know enough about it; I don't have time to read outside 'my field.'"

Patricia Limerick has written: "Traced to their source, many of the complaints about multiculturalism stem from the fundamental fact that there is too much to read." She asks instructors and those concerned with curriculum to "recognize that much of the grumpiness currently aimed at studies of gender, race, class, and ethnicity is, in fact, a response to a vast, worldwide rush to publish information."[6]

The most important step in diversifying the curriculum is not necessarily adding new information, but applying critical thinking to what is already being taught. It is vital to recognize that multiculturalism is as much about ways of thinking and teaching as it is about specific information. Furthermore, critical thinking is an area in which all academics are experts. Not that information is unnecessary; certainly it is essential. But many of those who believe they cannot provide a culturally diverse approach in the classroom because they lack expertise also say, "One of the things I like about teaching is that you learn so much." If, indeed, teaching is seen as a learning experience, then attempting to incorporate multiculturalism is a true opportunity to learn something new.

"Diversity is better covered in specialized courses."

Diversity is about thinking, but it is also about accuracy. Introductory courses are meant to give the basics. If the basics do not include all peoples and all parts of the world, then we are providing an inadequate—indeed, an inaccurate—base for more advanced study. Information about the forces which shaped governmental policies toward nineteenth-century Chinese immigrants, about the role of women's associations in supplying Civil War troops, or about the differences between slaves who came from east Africa and those who came from west Africa obviously will be provided in much greater depth in specialized courses. Nevertheless, advanced courses in every discipline should be able to assume that students have acquired basic information and basic approaches and attitudes in introductory courses.

"My syllabus is already too full; I can't add another unit."

The problem of not enough room in the syllabus is critical for many educators. A premise of this book is that changes and additions which will not totally alter an established syllabus are possible and can be meaningful. Since no semester is ever long enough to cover all that the instructor would like to include, choices are always necessary. In making those choices, the instructor can give priority to topics or approaches which would provide opportunities for thinking about issues related to diversity.

In addition, some instructors may want to consider the old question: "Am I teaching history or am I teaching students?" Acknowledging that the student, rather than the subject matter, is the more important element in the teaching/learning equation may make it possible for the thoughtful instructor to sacrifice just a bit of the traditional syllabus in order to provide a broader—and thus, ultimately, a more meaningful and accurate—view of the subject.

PLAN OF THE BOOK

Part I of this book contains specific, practical ideas designed to be useful to instructors in all disciplines who are looking for strategies to incorporate diversity into their courses.

Chapter 1 examines objectives and priorities, the structuring of syllabi, and the use of appropriate language.

Chapter 2 enumerates and discusses specific classroom strategies which can add diversity.

Chapter 3 addresses the selection of topics for diversity-related student projects and methods of structuring those projects for maximum effectiveness. Suggestions for working effectively with the library are also included.

Chapter 4 describes an assortment of specific formats which can be used for students to report the results of their research, reading, and thinking. Projects which do not require library research are included along with those which do. The emphasis is on flexibility in the amount of time required of both student and instructor. The chapter concludes with a note on student plagiarism.

Chapter 5 considers possible problems which might arise when introducing this material to the class. Some helpful approaches to these problems are also suggested.

Part II of this book is devoted to information resources and research strategies that can assist the instructor in broadening the curriculum and in devising student projects, and will be useful to students undertaking those projects.

Chapter 6 provides an annotated list of sources, ranging from encyclopedias to archives.

Chapter 7 discuses the complexity of Library of Congress subject headings and includes hints for the efficient use of an online catalog.

NOTES

1. Lawrence W. Levine, "Clio, Canons, and Culture," *Journal of American History* 88 (December 1993): 853.

2. Ibid., 866.

3. These stages are discussed frequently in the literature. For a brief bibliography and a useful summary see American Council on Education, *Minorities on Campus: A Handbook for Enhancing Diversity,* edited by Madeleine F. Green (Washington, DC, 1989), pp. 149–151.

4. Henry Louis Gates, Jr., "Beware the New Pharaohs," *Newsweek*, September 23, 1991, p. 46.

5. This issue is discussed in James A. Banks, *Teaching Strategies for Ethnic Studies,* 5th ed. (Boston: Allyn and Bacon, 1991), pp. 501–506; Raymond Frey, "Can a White Professor Teach African-American History? A Personal Perspective," *Transformations* 4 (spring 1993): 45–49; Natan I. Huggins, "Integrating Afro-American History into American History," in Darlene Clark Hine, ed., *The State of Afro-American History: Past, Present and Future* (Baton Rouge: Louisiana State University Press, 1986), pp. 166–167.

6. Patricia Nelson Limerick, "Information Overload Is a Prime Factor in Our Cultural Wars," *Chronicle of Higher Education*, July 29, 1992, p. A32.

I
Strategies

1

Groundwork for a Multicultural Approach

This chapter discusses objectives and priorities, strategies for building a syllabus to incorporate multicultural objectives, and the use of appropriate language.

OBJECTIVES AND PRIORITIES

Instructors generally have two sets of objectives for their students: achieving mastery and understanding of a set of facts and ideas, and developing the basic academic skills of reading, writing, research, and critical thinking. To these basic objectives, some instructors are now adding a new objective: helping students achieve a multicultural perspective on what they are learning.

The problem with this new objective is that it is last on the list. And how often does anyone deal effectively with "last on the list"? One way to approach the problem is to make diversity an overall umbrella and then look at everything being done as a potential area for incorporating it. At some points in the syllabus, diversity will not be appropriate; at others it will. But one will not find those places where it will work unless the inclusion of diversity becomes a priority rather than "last on the list."

Once having established diversity as a priority, the instructor has two choices: Make the objective explicit to the class or take a more subtle approach.[1] The more subtle, implicit approach to the incorporation of multiculturalism into the curriculum will be preferred by some instructors. The subtle approach averts the possibility of initial hostility on the part of students and permits the introduction of such material as gradually and as minimally as the instructor wishes. The problem with this approach is that unless the concepts are totally integrated they are more likely to become just "interesting asides" to the class and to not be taken seriously.

The arguments in favor of the explicit approach are clear. The very statement of diversity as an objective of the course tells students that it is important. It will communicate to women and to students from minority groups that their concerns are of concern to you. It can also help establish a classroom in which all students will feel comfortable raising questions. Furthermore, making the objective explicit to the class might make it easier for the instructor not to forget it.

Although the second alternative may sound more difficult and be viewed as having a greater potential for early confrontations with students, it is ultimately more honest than the first and may even be easier because it leaves the way open for a higher level of student participation in the process.

Whichever approach is preferred, the key point is that the objective of incorporating diversity into the curriculum—even in small amounts— must become a priority, not just another objective. It may be helpful, however, to view the achievement of this objective as a long-term process. Thus, while recognizing the importance of turning objectives into priorities, one can still start small and build gradually.

CONTENT OF THE SYLLABUS

Many approaches and strategies are available for the nonspecialist attempting to add diversity while not totally changing the accustomed course content or structure. Several are discussed below.

Asking the Questions

The most important step in making the curriculum more inclusive is not adding more material but thinking about the problems and asking the questions. Regardless of discipline, all faculty are (or should be) experts in the process of critical thinking.

In reviewing the content of the course, question every generalization. Look critically at everything to be taught and ask in what way it could be changed to reflect a more inclusive reality. Find questions to ask which are outside the traditional disciplinary boxes. Then, having looked at existing opportunities for including a more diverse approach, consider the possibility of adding opportunities for that approach.

Developing Reading Lists to Reflect Diversity

Many instructors routinely design reading lists to reflect opposing points of view. By consciously striving for diversity, the instructor can broaden this approach to include ideas and groups that have traditionally been considered so peripheral that they were not even considered for an "opposing" view. Readings which include feminist critiques of Freud, views of the political system from the perspective of the poor and disenfranchised, and the history of westward expansion through the eyes of Native Americans are just a few obvious examples.

If the objective is not only to provide students with diverse approaches to the subject matter, but also to make it clear that this diversity of approach is important, you may wish to discuss this fact with the class when you distribute the reading list.

Reading lists can also reflect diversity in authorship. The fact that the author is female or Chicano—even if the gender or ethnicity does not appear to be reflected in the content—is an important point to make to today's diverse student body.

If you think diversity of authorship is important, why not point it out to the students? Even in cases where ethnicity is clearly reflected in a name, many people have difficulty determining the gender of African and Asian given names. Remember also that scholarly documentation in the sciences and in those publications which follow the American Psychological Association style manual does not include given names. As a result, the gender of the author is not evident.

Several approaches can be used to alter or expand reading lists so that both contents and authors reflect a measure of diversity. One does not need to become an instant expert in ethnic, global, or feminist studies to start the process.

- As a first step, you might do what you probably already do when you need a reference in your own work: Call a colleague. A request to the chair of the women studies department or Chicano studies department will almost certainly be met with interest, respect, and concrete suggestions or a referral to the best-qualified member of the department. The truth is, most of us like to parade our knowledge before an appreciative audience, and who could be more appreciative than another academic! Institutions which don't have specific departments in these areas almost always have experts on them within the traditional departments.

- Consult a librarian. If there is a subject bibliographer for women studies or ethnic studies within the library, that person can probably furnish some useful suggestions. If there is no such specialist, ask the chief librarian or the head of reference for help. Your results will probably be better if you don't wait until the last minute to make your request.

- Do some browsing in the library yourself. Consult Chapter 7 for suggestions on key word and subject searching in the online catalog.

- Get some recent catalogs from publishers who specialize in minority and women studies. See Appendix B for a list of these publishers.

- Many professional associations now have divisions or committees concerned with issues of multiculturalism, and some of these have issued extremely useful publications. Contact the relevant ones to find out about such publications and also to make helpful contacts within your discipline.

- If there is no time for you to make changes, discuss the problem with your students. It is possible to enlist their help either by turning the expansion of the bibliography into an assigned research project or by offering extra credit for students who locate useful additions to your bibliography.

- Finally, if you (or your students) cannot find materials written by women or members of minority groups or cannot find sources reflecting a diversity of approaches to your subject, ask, why not? The answer may be as simple as using the wrong terminology in a library search or not recognizing that books from small publishers don't always find a place in mainstream bibliographies, or it may be as complex as reasons for the small number of women in physics or the need to redefine art in order to find women artists.

Just opening up the issue makes a significant point. Telling the class about your efforts and discussing the possible reasons for the lack of success could constitute a major step in raising awareness and sensitivity. It might also lead to further inquiries into the history of higher education, to greater awareness of subtle as well as overt prejudices, and to some sense of the powerful nature of established norms.

Evaluating the Textbook

Instructors generally rely on a required textbook or book of readings to provide basic facts and a common base of information for class discussions, student papers, and other readings. Students tend to accept the textbook as gospel, to assume that everything in it is accurate, and to believe that it fully reflects the point of view of the instructor. Given that students have had at least twelve years of relying on textbooks prior to appearing in college classrooms, generalized disclaimers about the nature of textbooks cannot by themselves totally change this view.

Although in recent years the publishing industry has responded to the movement for multiculturalism, finding appropriate textbooks can still be difficult. In assessing textbooks the instructor will naturally look at the diversity of information presented in both text and illustrations and read the text carefully for hidden biases and stereotypes. Few textbooks today are guilty of overt antiminority sentiments, but many contain subtle antifeminist or anti-immigrant statements, and even more still hew to the traditional view of the centrality of the white, Eurocentric, upper-class world.

Numerous anthologies or books of readings with multicultural themes are available for college courses, and many instructors adopt these as supplements to the textbook. In selecting and assigning such an anthology, however, it is well to be alert to two potential dangers inherent in many of these books. It can be misleading to allow a single selection to represent an entire culture or approach, and—particularly in the case of composition readers—there is frequently an overreliance on personal narratives, many of which present the authors as victims.[2]

None of the above means that instructors who have found texts and anthologies which meet the needs of their syllabus in all areas other than diversity cannot appropriately continue to use those books. What is essential is to discuss the omissions and drawbacks with the students and to attempt to make up for them in some other way.

Rearranging the Syllabus Around Broad Themes

Some faculty, faced with the difficulty of moving away from a Eurocentric approach or of incorporating the viewpoints of women and minorities into their courses, have reported that organizing course content by themes rather than by the more traditional chronological or "great thinkers" approaches has been successful. For example, one teacher of theology describes changing from a study of Barth, Brunner, Tillich, and Niebuhr to a study of topics such as the interpretation of sin, human redemption, and the conception of God. The change allowed for broader readings and discussion. Small groups did biographical studies and made short oral reports about the key theologians on whom the course previously centered.[3] Other instructors have found this approach useful in fields as diverse as American literature and political theory.[4]

Redesigning Student Assignments

The multicultural approaches to which you would like students to become sensitive can become the basis of student projects such as those described in Chapters 3 and 4. Just the inclusion of a diversity-related topic on the list of suggested projects—even if no one chooses to write on it—signals that it is a legitimate subject for research. If you prefer to insure a multicultural experience for all students, all the suggested topics can in some way reflect diversity.

LANGUAGE, WORDS, AND NAMES

Language is central to issues of communication and learning and the most basic tool of teaching. A form of social behavior which reflects cultural beliefs and biases, language is a potent tool in subconsciously establishing and perpetuating norms. Among the easiest ways to increase sensitivity to diversity in the classroom is to heighten awareness of the subtle biases carried in language. There is nothing radical or difficult here; it is a question of being alert to implied or hidden meanings in everyday words and phrases.[5]

Rosalie Maggio points out that "bias-free language is logical, accurate, and realistic; biased language is not."[6] She delineates several ways in which bias occurs in language:

- Unintentionally leaving out individuals and/or groups, as in the note: "Employees are welcome to bring their wives and children."

- Calling individuals or groups by names or labels they do not choose for themselves, as in referring to the Romany people as "gypsies" or assuming that Juan would be happy to be called "John."

- Stereotypical treatment that implies everyone in a group is alike, as in "Asian students are all naturally good at mathematics" or "People on welfare lack the initiative to find jobs."

- Unequal specification of aggregate groups, as in "the French and the Asians" rather than "the Europeans and the Asians" or "the French and the Japanese."

- Unnecessary mention of membership in a particular group when it is not relevant, as in "Anna Frascatti, sixty-five years old and a grand-mother, was promoted to general manager."

- Not giving the person preference over the qualifier, as in "a diabetic," or "a cripple" rather than "a person with diabetes" or "a person with a disability."

Appropriate and aware use of language is a subtle yet powerful way of breaking down biases and stereotypes of gender, class, and race.

Gender and Language

The question of gender bias in language has been discussed a great deal in recent years. Most academics have become adjusted to the modifications made to render the use of language more accurate, and they now routinely refer to chairpersons rather than chairmen and to police officers rather than policemen. However, there are still areas in which such adjustments have not occurred or have been inadequate.[7]

In looking at these other areas, useful distinctions can be made among (1) terms which include everyone (workers, people, we, they), (2) terms which could include everyone but are usually assumed to describe men (pilot, doctor), and (3) terms that are used as if they include everyone but in reality do not (mankind, forefathers, he to mean he or she).

In many cases, accuracy can be achieved by using terms which are either gender-free (patient, people, workers) or gender-specific (Councilwoman Jones and Councilman Alfonso; Kisha the altar girl and Georgio the altar boy). Problems arise, however, in the use of terms which, although appearing to apply to everyone, are automatically thought of as being male (and probably white and middle-class as well). Quickly picture in your mind (or ask your class to do it) a lawyer, a pilot, a member of the clergy, a farmer, a president, a pioneer, a business executive. The pictures which come to mind, in addition to almost invariably being male, tend to confirm other stereotypes: The executive will never be a person in a wheelchair; the pilot will always be white; and no person with any prestige is likely to look sixty-five years old![8]

How can we overcome this? One approach is to always specify gender unless the context or the name makes it clear. Referring to Dr. Alvarez as a male doctor sends a signal that Dr. Alvarez might have been female. It may sound strange but that is a small price to pay in efforts to overcome centuries of prejudice and stereotypes.

Perhaps the most ubiquitous gender bias in the English language is the use of the word "he" to stand for "he and she." Thus, one reads that "the doctor . . . he," "the politician . . . he," and "the professor . . . he." It is impossible to estimate how many times in a lifetime speakers of English hear this construction. More important, how many times do young children, who are never told that in some instances he means he and she, hear this construction, absorb its subtle biases, and come to see maleness as being the generally accepted state of being and femaleness as being peripheral or outside the norm?

If one is sensitive to the problem, the use of the generic "he" can be avoided. A sentence can be restructured into the plural to permit the use of "they" as the referent (there appears to be a move among some grammarians to solve the problem by allowing the use of "they" with a singular antecedent). "One" can be utilized, or a truly generic noun can be substituted for the pronoun, or one can use "he or she." Similarly, the use of words like "mankind" and "brotherhood" can be eschewed in favor of synonyms such as "all people" or "everyone."

Bias in Labels and Descriptions

If we are to present a truly equitable worldview, we must look carefully at much of our generally accepted terminology. Every schoolchild learns that Columbus discovered America. The concept that no one knew about the existence of North America before his voyage immediately makes the original inhabitants of the area something less than people; it reinforces that the norm for the word "people" is "white Europeans." If one said that Columbus landed in America, it might be viewed as value-free, although some people feel that the use of the term "invade" would be more accurate. Similarly, we read of "the era of westward expansion" where Native Americans might say "the era of the great invasion."

Who is included? Who is excluded? Coming to grips with definitions of words like "civilization," "world," "culture," and "American" is critical; like the generic "he" they need to be used accurately. If a course is called "World History," it should consider the entire world. There is nothing wrong with teaching the literature or history of Europe as long as it is labeled correctly. A course labeled "Art Appreciation and History" should consider a selection of all forms of art from all over the world and should not be limited to high art of the Western world. We should reach the point where if we mean Europe and the United States, we call it that clearly; in the absence of such specificity, one should be able to assume that the whole world is included.

Be alert also to biases and insensitivities which may be hidden in the use of aggregate nouns. Speaking about Asian Americans may be appropriate if one also speaks about European Americans. However, if the distinction between German and British is recognized, so should the distinction between

Japanese and Vietnamese. The immigrant from the Dominican Republic is as different from the one from Haiti as is the Irish person from the Scottish. Although many people will defend the use of aggregate terms such as Hispanic or Asian as being only a convenient way to make a grouping, the alert educator should be aware that the use of such terms is frequently the result of a lack of awareness that there are meaningful differences. Insensitive use of aggregate terms reinforces stereotypes.

Names

People's names are important to them. It is a simple matter for instructors to show respect for diversity in the classroom by acknowledging the significance of names, knowing how to pronounce them, and recognizing the components of name forms in languages other than English. It is also important for students to learn to pronounce each other's names. In a multicultural classroom, it will provide at least the first step in their establishing relationships with each other, and help to remove the awkwardness which can arise when attempting the unfamiliar sounds of names from unfamiliar cultures.

Name forms are complex. In languages and cultures with which we are familiar, we rely on common knowledge to know that Susan is a given name and Smith and Brown are family names. Even when seeing Susan Smith Brown, we feel reasonably confident in addressing her as Ms. Brown, even though there is a possibility that she prefers Ms. Smith Brown. Although we may recognize the symbolic importance of being able to call a student by the proper name, when dealing with unfamiliar languages and cultures, we lack this common knowledge and familiarity. One suggestion for overcoming the difficulty is this: When first meeting a class, read each student's name aloud in its full uninverted form even if the registrar (or the registrar's computer) has provided a surname-first list. The student can then be asked the proper name form, and the instructor can be spared having said it wrong.

The following brief discussion of name forms is intended only as a general guide; as with names derived from European countries, there are few fast rules and many exceptions.

Hispanic Names. People of Latin American heritage frequently have three or more elements in their names.[9] The personal name is clear: It is either first or immediately after a comma if an inverted form is used. How to address the person in a formal situation is more complex.

A single woman will have a personal name, her father's family name, and her mother's family name. For example, in the name MARIA PICO

BELLIN, Maria is the personal name, Pico is the father's family name, and Bellin is the mother's family name. In most cases a woman is referred to by the father's family name; in this instance she will be addressed as MS. PICO. In very formal situations, however, she may be addressed as MS. PICO BELLIN, but never as MS. BELLIN.

A woman who marries has several options today: If Ms. Pico marries Mr. Hernandez, she may adopt the traditional form of name, MARIA PICO DE HERNANDEZ; use the more modern form, MARIA PICO-HER-NANDEZ; or choose to remain as MARIA PICO BELLIN. In all of these cases, she is most appropriately addressed as MS. PICO, although strict traditionalists may prefer MRS. PICO DE HERNANDEZ or MS. PICO-HERNANDEZ.

JULIO HERNANDEZ SANCHEZ, whose father is Mr. Hernandez and whose mother was Ms. Sanchez before she got married, is always referred to as MR. HERNANDEZ.

Arabic Names. Arabic names are similar to Hispanic names in the tradition of carrying personal name, father's family name, and often the mother's family name.[10]

Most people of Arabic heritage in the United States follow U.S. custom and choose to be addressed in formal situations by their father's name. Thus, ISMAIL HUSSEIN is called MR. HUSSEIN. In some places and situations in Arabic countries, however, people are addressed by their personal name and not by their father's name. Thus, GAMIL IBRAHIM, (Gamil being his given name, and Ibrahim being his father's family name) would be called GAMIL in informal situations but might be called MR. GAMIL in some formal ones. In a formal written communication, he will be called MR. GAMIL IBRAHIM. A woman, when she marries, might not adopt her husband's name, but will change the designation: MISS NABI-LAH AHMAD might become MRS. NABILAH AHMAD and in some situations and countries might be called MRS. NABILAH. Adaptations made by women of Arabic heritage in the United States vary.

Several prefixes are common in Arabic names. *Ibn* means "son of"; MOHAMMAD IBN SAUD is the son of Mr. Saud and is called either MR. MOHAMMAD or MR. IBN SAUD. *Abdul* (male) or its abbreviation *Abd'*, and *Amat* (female) mean "servant or worshipper of." They are always used as prefixes if a person has been named after a prophet and are always part of the name by which the person is addressed. Thus, YOUSSIF ABDUL RAHIM is called either MR. YOUSSIF or MR. ABDUL RAHIM. In many cases the prefix and the name are written as one word (ABDULRAHIM).

Chinese Names. If it sometimes seems as if an unusual number of Chinese students have the same names, it is because there are only about two hundred family names in common use, and only a little over two thousand altogether.[11]

If Chinese names are written traditionally, the surname comes first without any punctuation to separate it from given names. Thus, CHU WU LAI is MR. CHU in formal situations and WU LAI to his friends. In American classrooms, the difficulty arises because we don't know if the particular person has Americanized the manner in which the name is written.

The most popular Chinese surnames are Chang, Chao, Chen, Chu, Ho, Hsu, Hu, Li, Liu, Wang, and Wu. If any of these are part of the name, they can safely be assumed to be surnames; also, as a general rule, surnames are one syllable, and when a hyphen is used it connects the middle name with the personal name. Thus, TANG TA-TAO is MR. TANG, as is TANG, TA-TAO. When the three parts are written without a hyphen, generalization is more difficult.

Japanese Names. As in Chinese, the Japanese family name comes before the personal name, and there are relatively few family names.[12] Among the most popular are Ito, Saito, Takahashi, Tamura, Tanaka, Watanabe, and Yamamoto. If one of these appears, either first or last, it can be assumed to be the family name.

Pronunciation of Names. It is nice to be able to properly pronounce people's names the first time you address them. There are many books available which were written to help people select names for their children; in recent years, many of these books have been addressed to particular ethnic groups. The books generally carry simple pronunciation guides. Although unlikely to be in the college library, this kind of publication will be available in the public library.

A more direct approach is to hear correct pronunciations from the students themselves. If the class is not too large, students can be asked to introduce themselves to the rest of the class by saying their names aloud slowly and distinctly. This could be done not only on the first day of class, but over several more days, until you and your students have learned the correct pronunciations. If this direct approach is used, those students who wish to could also tell their classmates where they were born and if they are fortunate enough to know any languages other than English. Sharing this very basic information could increase the multicultural awareness of the students in the class and also alert the instructor to backgrounds and abilities which might be called upon to broaden the overall perspective of the course.

NOTES

1. For one discussion of this dilemma, see Joan Rothschild, *Teaching Technology from a Feminist Perspective: A Practical Guide* (New York: Pergamon Press, 1988), pp. 32–38.

2. This was well pointed out by Nancy Shapiro in an untitled lengthy review article on several college composition readers, which appeared in *College Composition and Communication* 42 (December 1991): 526.

3. Elaine R. Ognibene, "Integrating the Curriculum: From Impossible to Possible," *College Teaching* 37 (summer 1989): 107–108.

4. For political theory see Bernice Carroll, "Transforming the Malestream . . . Integrating Women's Studies into the Political Science Curriculum," in Myra Dinnerstein and Betty Schmitz, eds., *Ideas and Resources for Integrating Women's Studies into the Curriculum,* 2 vols. (Tucson: University of Arizona Press, 1986).

5. For a short but useful discussion of this issue, see Rosalie Maggio, *The Dictionary of Bias-free Usage: A Guide to Nondiscriminatory Language* (Phoenix, AZ: Oryx, 1991). For a more extensive discussion and an excellent bibliography, see Lourdes Torres, "Women and Language," in Cheris Kramarae and Dale Spender, eds., *The Knowledge Explosion: Generations of Feminist Scholarship* (New York: Teachers College Press, 1992).

6. Maggio, *The Dictionary of Bias-free Usage*, p. 5.

7. There is an interesting discussion of gender and language, along with additional citations to the literature, in Barrie Thorne, "Rethinking the Ways We Teach," in Carol S. Pearson, Donna L. Shavlik, and Judith G. Touchton, eds., *Educating the Majority: Women Challenge Tradition in Higher Education* (New York: American Council on Education and Macmillan Publishing, 1989).

8. An interesting exercise dealing with stereotypes is described by Phyllis Bronstein and Michele Paludi in "The Introductory Psychology Course from a Broader Human Perspective," in Phyllis Bronstein and Katheryn Quina, eds., *Teaching a Psychology of People: Resources for Gender and Sociocultural Awareness* (Washington, DC: American Psychological Association, 1988), pp. 30–31. A paragraph is distributed to the class describing an incident in which a woman saw a UFO and reported it to the police. Students are asked to decide whether the woman actually saw a UFO, whether she saw some natural phenomenon and not a UFO, whether she imagined the entire episode, or whether she made it all up to get attention. The entire class gets the same questions and the same description except that for one-third of the class the woman is described as age twenty-eight; for another third she is described as age sixty-eight; and for the final group no age is given but she is described as being in a wheelchair.

9. I am indebted to Dr. Altagracia Ortiz of John Jay College of Criminal Justice for much of the explanation in this section.

10. I am indebted to Mr. Gamil Youssef of the Oriental Division of the New York Public Library for much of the information in this section.

11. Elsdon C. Smith, *Treasure of Name Lore* (New York: Harper & Row, 1967), p. 39.

12. Information from "Names" in *Japan: An Illustrated Encyclopedia*, 2 vols. (Tokyo: Kodansha, 1993).

2

Classroom Strategies: Activities and Resources to Add Diversity

This chapter describes specific useful, simple, and practical classroom activities and resources which can be used to enhance diversity without making major changes in an established syllabus.

WHO SITS WHERE?

Most instructors would like to see students of various ethnic groups establish a rapport with each other in class. Too often, however, we see a kind of instinctive self-segregation as students wander in on the first day of class and sit next to those they already know or those of their own group with whom they automatically feel more comfortable.

One simple way to counteract this habitual behavior is to have students sit alphabetically. At the start of the first class the instructor could ask students to stand up, introduce themselves, and arrange themselves in alphabetical order. The small amount of chaos thus engendered might put students more at ease with each other while enabling them (and the instructor) to learn the names—and the pronunciation of those names—of their classmates. In the end, the instructor will have an arrangement which will make it easier to remember students' names and one which will provide the possiblity of a small step toward intergroup understanding on a personal level.

In classes which will be doing small-group work, if the groups are arbitrary and not based on the selection of topics by the students, the alphabetically arranged classroom is more likely to result in diversity within the small groups.

POWER OF THE FIRST EXAMPLE

The first unit taught can be a natural referent for all future ideas presented. Thus, if the first assigned reading or the first class discussion focuses even partially on an issue related to diversity, the basis will be laid for such references later in the semester.

GUEST SPEAKERS

A fairly obvious way to add diversity is to invite speakers who represent other points of view or speakers from minority groups who will speak on traditional topics. It is important not to overlook the second point: speakers who are members of minority groups should not always be equated with minority interests.

To avoid the embarrassing silence when the speaker asks for questions, the instructor can have students prepared ahead of time. Students can take responsibility for orchestrating the entire session with the guest. Before the speaker comes, they can discuss potential questions and decide together which ones to ask the guest. In some cases it might work well to form a student panel to ask the questions.[1]

Alternatively, before announcing a guest speaker, the instructor can structure class discussion around a question such as "If you could ask a person who is Native American about this event, what would you ask?" or "How would a description of this by a woman born in Japan vary from what we have been discussing?" At the conclusion of the discussion, announce the guest speaker. In any case, be sure that students are aware of the qualifications of the speaker and, if possible, have read some of his or her works.

FILMS AND VIDEOS

One of the most effective ways to add diversity to a course is through the use of appropriate films and videos. Although many instructors routinely integrate films and videos into their courses, others do not. Reasons for not doing so vary:

- Scheduling a film might be viewed by others as an excuse not to teach that day.
- The equipment is unfamiliar and the instructor is reluctant to deal with it.
- The instructor lacks information about suitable films.
- The instructor may not want to reinforce students' overuse of video.

The appropriate use of films is an acknowledgment that people learn in different ways. Although many are firmly wedded to the printed word, information contained in a film is fully as valid as that contained in a book, and today's video generation is more accustomed to absorbing information from films and videos than from any other format.

It must be made clear to students that the film or video is being shown for educational reasons. Students need to be taught how to *watch* critically just as much as they need to be taught how to *read* critically. They need to understand that the way in which the film is made—the camera angles, the framing of the scenes, the amount of light, the choice of costume and background, the type of music—influences the conclusions to be drawn just as much as do the words and the way in which they are spoken. Of course, if students are to see the film as education, the instructor will want to be present when it is shown; otherwise, it will be interpreted as unimportant.

Deirdre Boyle, who teaches in the graduate Media Studies Program at the New School for Social Research in New York City, firmly maintains that the "best way to jog the viewer out of the passivity induced by years of watching television" is to insist that students take notes while watching the video.[2] Although this may sound a bit difficult, students can learn to do it. (Reviewers and students of media routinely do so.) The need to take notes when watching focuses the attention in the same way as that need focuses the attention when reading. It also sharply differentiates the film watched for learning from the film watched for entertainment.

If at all possible, videotapes should be selected over film. Because they allow the easy use of stop-frame, search, and replay, videos make analysis and discussion easier in the classroom. The technology is also more familiar, and even if the instructor is not thoroughly familiar with the idiosyncrasies of video players, there is sure to be a student in the class who is.

In looking for films and videos to add diversity to the curriculum, instructors should consider going beyond the usual commercial and educational products to those which are independently made and produced. Women and members of minority groups who are independent videomakers can provide a different viewpoint, can speak with a different voice, and can display a commitment and passion which may be missing from commercial documentaries and bland "objective" educational films. *Mediating History: The MAP Guide to Independent Video by and about African American, Asian American, Latino, and Native American People* is an excellent guide to these sources. It contains essays about these videos, discussions on how to use them in class, and lists of directories to aid in selecting and locating them.[3]

In selecting commercially made videos and films, don't overlook productions from other countries. After students read a play by Shakespeare and perhaps view a British or American production, for example, it would be interesting for them to see sections of a Russian or Spanish production. Although students will not understand the words spoken, they will know the content and context and be able to see the differences in production. Similarly, classes reading Cervantes or Balzac in translation can see selections from native-language productions after viewing English-language ones. Such use of the dramatic and cinematic productions of other countries can reinforce for students that much of what we consider great in world literature is also considered great in other parts of the world.

Although films probably need to be shown in class, in many institutions the library or media center has provisions for individual and small-group viewing of videos, making it possible to assign them for viewing out of class. Several related videos can be assigned to predetermined groups of students who can then report back to the class. A selection of relevant videos can also be put on reserve for the semester, with each student required to select one or two to view.

The section "Visual Sources" in Chapter 6 describes sources which will be useful in selecting and obtaining both independently produced and commercial videos and films.

TIME-LINES

An effective and graphic way to counteract the prevailing Eurocentric view of the world is the use of global time-lines, devices which can also help students develop a sense of historical continuity. The time-line can be designed to show political and economic developments, cultural or technological developments, or characteristics of everyday life on each continent at a particular time in history. Topics as diverse as the New Deal, Shakespeare, Beethoven, and the discoveries of Sir Isaac Newton would benefit from the international and historical perspective provided by such a graphic presentation.

Useful time-lines of a general type are available from suppliers of educational materials for secondary schools. By utilizing and combining the chronologies available in various reference books, instructors can devise their own time-lines which will be more relevant to the specific course.[4] The time-lines can be designed to show events by year, decade, or century, depending on the course. They can be made as posters and left to hang as a constant silent reminder, or they can be made as notebook-sized sheets and distributed to the students.

MAPS AND GLOBES

It is vital for citizens of the global world in the twenty-first century to comprehend fully the political and physical sizes, distances, and proximities of places on the earth. A globe large enough to show every country and physical feature in the world clearly to someone sitting several feet away would be the best way to accomplish this goal but that is obviously an impossibility. Within the average classroom the best we can do is to expose students to a changing array of graphic representations of the boundaries and physical features of the world.

It is essential that students be made aware that maps, as representations of reality, are drawn to serve specific purposes. "Every map shows *this* . . . but not *that*, and every map shows what it shows this *way* . . . but not *the other*."[5] How many subtle messages does a graphic representation of the world carry? If one always sees North America or Europe at the center of a map, does it unconsciously influence one's thinking about the world? A map with Asia in the center presents a different view of the planet. Or consider the equator, which we know is equidistant from the two poles. How many people are aware that the average (Mercator projection) flat map of the world does not place the equator in the middle of the page? In order to minimize the distortion effect on western Europe, Mercator (living and working in Germany) moved the equator below the center, thus allowing a "clearer" presentation of western Europe and disproportionately "shrinking" South America and Africa.

A variety of maps can be used to increase the global sensitivity of students. The projections of Arno Peters, which are drawn with the emphasis on fidelity in presenting the relative sizes of land masses, are particularly interesting and useful.[6]

Atlases can lead to even greater misperceptions about relative sizes of countries than wall maps cause. Of course, each page of an atlas needs to be the same size as every other page. When each country is then allotted one page in the atlas, it obviously means that each map is then drawn to a different scale. Thus, one becomes accustomed to seeing Japan and China each on one page and England and Australia each on one page. Again, the Peters atlas, with representations of countries of the world in individual maps drawn to the same scale, is highly recommended. It is truly an eye-opener!

If an understanding of the physical world is important in any way to the context of the course, it is appropriate that map exercises be included in the syllabus and that map questions be included on exams. Even if maps seem totally irrelevant to a particular course, consider requesting that one be hung permanently in the classroom. Who knows, the inattentive student staring out the window might just study the map instead and at least learn some geography.

USING THE FIRST FIVE MINUTES

Faculty in all disciplines have devised imaginative ways to utilize the first five minutes of class. Rather than sacrifice the time for just settling down, some instructors have exploited those precious minutes to further their diversity objectives.

One teacher of American literature, for example, disturbed that the chronological approach she was accustomed to using did not present any women authors during the first half of the semester, told the students that she would begin each class by reading a poem by Emily Dickinson, her favorite author. Since the poem was not discussed, this reading took under five minutes. Sometimes the poem was related to the topic to be discussed that day; more often it was not. But there was a woman's literary voice in every class; and by the time the class got to Dickinson, they were more prepared than they otherwise would have been.[7] Readings from diaries of working people or political prisoners; letters from immigrants; observations by politicians from other countries; and reflections by scientists, mathematicians, or novelists could all be used for these five-minute diversity-related readings. (If the passages read will not come up in the course of the classwork, it might be appropriate at some point to provide students with written copies of the readings.)

The first five minutes can also be used to relate some facts from the history of your discipline. This would be particularly useful in mathematics and science to introduce the broader perspectives which underlie these disciplines and to show that they are not just numbers and the manipulation of measurable data.

Instructors can also use this brief period to present biographical information about some of the people who have contributed to the discipline. Students who normally associate science or philosophy only with men or Europeans can be introduced to others who have made significant contributions. Those who think all science is associated with high-technology laboratories can be told of scientific discoveries made in earlier times. If the professor runs out of examples, students can be challenged to find some.

Some instructors have found the use of media effective in setting the mood for a class during its first five minutes. A short slide show—Winslow Homer woodcuts of the Civil War, photographs of migrant laborers or of

Native American reservations, a montage of eighteenth-century quilts—can set the tone for the day. It is perhaps easier, in terms of equipment, to play an audiocassette tape of Malcolm X delivering a speech, a performance of Native American music or union organizing songs, or folk songs related to the era or subject. Any of these would catch students' attention and focus them on the lecture or discussion which is to follow.[8]

AN UNUSUAL USE OF THE CHALKBOARD

Similar, but a bit more passive, is the strategy of utilizing the chalkboard to provide a bit of interesting information. One instructor reports an experiment with quotations: He adopted the practice of putting a quotation on the board every day before class. Although not always relevant to the course content, the quotations were carefully chosen for general appeal and interest. The class came to look forward to them and complained when the daily quotation was missing.[9]

The same strategy can be adapted to present information related in some way to the subject of the class: facts from the history of the discipline, brief biographies, and statistics. As with the oral presentations described above, a mathematics instructor can use the chalkboard to provide information from the field of ethnomathematics; a science class can get data about indigenous science systems; brief bits of information about the history of science can alternate with biographical information about women scientists overlooked in the standard works; and statistics and comparative information from other countries can point the way to more global viewpoints on almost any subject. After a few weeks of the instructor's supplying these comments, students could be offered extra credit for supplying their own appropriate pieces of information.

THE BILINGUAL ADVANTAGE

If there are bilingual students in the class who would not feel uncomfortable in the role, turn their bilingualism into an enriching factor for the entire class. Ask them how key concepts are described in the other language: Is it a direct translation? Are there subtle differences in the meanings of the words or in the viewpoint they convey? Some students may need to get the answers from parents or relatives and may thus enrich their own knowledge of their first language.

The editor of the journal *Teaching Tolerance*, disturbed by the dual meaning of the word "tolerance" in English, asked colleagues for translations into other languages. In Hindi, "tolerance" translates as *vishwa bandhutva*, which means "universal brotherhood"; in Russian it translates as *tertimost*, meaning "endurance"; in German it translates as *Völkerver-ständigung*, meaning "people understanding."[10] In Hebrew the word is *sovlanut*, derived from *savlanut*, which means "patience."

INTERNATIONAL COMPARISONS

International comparisons can provide students with a broader under-standing of social and economic problems and can be used without turning a course into a comparative study. This can be done most easily with statistics and would be effective in any class in which reference is routinely made to "the number of people who . . . " The simplest and most effective way to do this would be to select a single country to compare and contrast with our country. Compile a list of the statistics which might be relevant, keep it handy, and keep referring to it. Use of statistics in this way would take only a few minutes, but it would serve as a reminder that our own country is not the center of the world. Additional benefits for the students and the instructor would probably result if the comparison country was one from which a number of the students in the class had emigrated. Sources for these kinds of statistics are described in the section "Statistics" of Chapter 6.

CHOOSING EXAMPLES AND ILLUSTRATIONS

When lecturing or constructing exam questions, the instructor can make a modest contribution to diversity objectives by selecting examples which illustrate the fact that not everyone is heterosexual or able to see, hear, or walk; that not everyone is of the same class or age; or that people belong to many kinds of family structures and households and hold a very wide variety of religious and ethical beliefs. In addition, when selecting experiments or surveys to point out examples of good or bad research studies, the instructor can use designs which consider race, gender, class, or religion.[11]

TAKING A POSITION

The instructor can provide a physical incentive in the classroom for students to think actively about a problem discussed either in a homework assignment or in a class session. Before students come to class, rearrange the chairs on three sides of the room and label the sides Yes, No, and Undecided. (It is helpful if the classroom has chalkboards on three sides; otherwise just hang signs.) Students must choose an area in which to sit, but are encouraged to move their chairs at any time that they change their opinion.[12] "Taking a position" is clearly useful when discussing contemporary events or when using case studies; it can also be useful in an analysis of historical events, such as John Brown's "raid."

BOOKS FROM OTHER TIMES AND OTHER PLACES

Consider using atypical textbooks as oppositional reading to enhance discussions of diversity. McGuffey's readers can be used in any nineteenth-century context; textbooks, mass-market books, and scholarly monographs from the early part of the twentieth century can also be used to illustrate how basic assumptions about people and their roles have changed. Equally interesting might be the use of contemporary textbooks from Great Britain, Canada, New Zealand, and the English-language educational systems in Africa, the Caribbean, and India. Such books could provide intriguing insights into the study of history, sociology, geography, literature, and most other subjects.

There is an interesting book published for the bicentennial celebration by the U.S. government which illustrates this idea. It reproduces the chapters on the American Revolution in secondary school history textbooks from thirteen countries.[13] Even the chapter headings are interesting: In the Mexican textbook the American Revolution is called "The Emancipation of the United States," in the Israeli textbook it is "The War of Liberation of the North American Colonies," and in the textbook from Great Britain the chapter is called, "The End of an Empire, 1775–1783." Indicative of how different countries draw their own lessons is the concluding paragraph in the textbook from Ghana. After saying that Great Britain learned a lesson from the loss of the thirteen colonies and treated the settlers in Canada and Australia better, it continues: "In their other colonies, however, the British repeated the mistake of keeping colonial rule for too long a time. This led to another revolution: the emergence of self-rule in the former Asian and African colonies."[14]

English-language books from Africa, including textbooks, can be found listed in the catalogs of the African Books Collective. Mass-market and scholarly books from most countries of the world can be located using *International Books in Print*.[15] See Appendix B for a list of publishers and distributors including those which can supply books from other countries.

NEWSPAPERS FROM OTHER COUNTRIES

Current English-language newspapers from around the world may be easier to locate than textbooks and perhaps easier to introduce into the classroom. Their use in any course discussing topics like contemporary world politics, terrorism, multinational business, international trade, and immigration and emigration—even reviews of current American movies—could add breadth and diversity to students' understanding of these topics.

Descriptions of English-language newspapers from other countries may be found in *Willings Press Guide*, described in the section "Periodicals" in Chapter 6. This guide's annotations include targeted audience and type of coverage, as well as price and subscription information. In situations where a subscription to a foreign newspaper seems too ambitious, instructors could consider a service which provides summaries of articles from foreign newspapers. *World Press Review* and *The European Press Survey* have the advantage of providing a broader range of sources since they include translations from other languages. However, they lack the immediacy of holding and using an actual newspaper and have the disadvantage of covering a limited number of preselected topics. [16]

CASE STUDIES

A case study is basically a narrative description of a situation which requires a decision or action of some kind. After reading or hearing the case, the group is asked to discuss it and to recommend an action or decision. Using cases to present ideas and information automatically provides an opportunity for introducing diversity. Equally important is the fact that cases provide that opportunity in such a way that controversial or sensitive ideas can come from the students rather than the instructor. To insure full participation, cases to be discussed should be read in class. The discussions then can take place either in small groups (with a designated reporter) or with the class as a whole.[17]

SMALL DIGRESSIONS

Be alert to opportunities to introduce diversity through awareness of issues and events which are raised in the news or on campus. These can be used for your comments, for general discussions, or for opportunities for students to be the presenters and share information about their own cultures or experiences with the class.[18]

NOTES

1. See Chet Meyers and Thomas B. Jones, *Promoting Active Learning: Strategies for the College Classroom* (San Francisco: Jossey-Bass, 1993), p. 136.

2. Dierdre Boyle, "Critical Doubts and Differences: Independent Video and Teaching History," in Barbara Abrash and Catherine Egan, eds., *Mediating History: The MAP Guide to Independent Video by and about African American, Asian American, Latino, and Native American People* (New York: New York University Press, 1992).

3. Abrash and Egan, *Mediating History*. A fuller description of this book will be found in the section "Visual Sources" in Chapter 6.

4. Useful chronologies will be found in James A. Banks, *Teaching Strategies for Ethnic Studies*, 5th ed. (Boston: Allyn and Bacon, 1991), and in several of the works discussed in the section "Chronologies and Atlases" in Chapter 6.

5. Denis Wood, *The Power of Maps* (New York: Guilford Press, 1992), p. 1 (emphasis in the original).

6. Arno Peters, *Peters Atlas of the World* (New York: Harper & Row, 1990). For a discussion of these principles, see Arno Peters, *Die Neue Kartographie/The New Cartography* (New York: Friendship Press, 1983).

7. Susan Van Dyne, "American Literature, 1820–1865," in Myra Dinnerstein and Betty Schmitz, eds., *Ideas and Resources for Integrating Women's Studies into the Curriculum*, 2 vols. (Tucson: University of Arizona Press, 1986), 2: 20.

8. Use of media to set the tone of a class is discussed in Peter Frederick, "Using Emotions in the Classroom," in Betty E. M. Ch'maj, ed., *Multicultural America: A Resource Book for Teachers of Humanities and American Studies: Syllabi, Essays, Projects, Bibliography* (Lanham, MD: University Press of America, 1993).

9. Neil F. Williams, "The Quote of the Day," *The Teaching Professor*, October, 1990, p. 5.

10. Sara Ballard, "Editors Note," *Teaching Tolerance*, spring 1994, p. 4.

11. See Donna Crawley and Martha Ecker, "Integrating Issues of Gender, Race, and Ethnicity into Experimental Psychology and Other Social Science Methodology Courses," *Women's Studies Quarterly* 18, nos. 1, 2 (1990): 105–116.

12. This process was described by Ron Chandonia, in *Innovation Abstracts* 13 (September 20, 1991).

13. U.S. Department of Education, *The American Revolution: Selections from Secondary School History Books of Other Nations* (Washington, DC: Government Printing Office, 1976).

14. Ibid., p. 38.

15. *International Books in Print* (New Providence, NJ: Bowker, annual). There are some who feel that much African publishing is still dominated by larger, international publishers, and although the examples used may be African, the outlook is less likely to be so. In Asia and Latin America, the publishing industries are better developed, and textbooks are more likely to reflect local needs and concerns. See Philip G. Altbach and Gail P. Kelly, eds., *Textbooks in the Third World: Policy, Content, and Context* (New York: Garland, 1988), p. 241.

16. *World Press Review: News and Views from Foreign Press* (New York) monthly; *The European Press Survey: The Best of the Press of Europe* (Albuquerque, NM) weekly.

17. I am indebted to Dr. Serena Nanda and Dr. Jill Norgren of John Jay College for their insights on the use of case studies.

18. Jonathan Collett and Basilio Serano assert that "the practice of taking time out of class to discuss current, especially controversial, issues, whether based on campus or world events, is characteristic of effective teachers." In "Stirring It Up: The Inclusive

Classroom," in Laura L. B. Border and Nancy Van Note Chism, eds., *Teaching for Diversity* (San Francisco: Jossey-Bass, 1992), p. 46.

3

Strategies and Resources for Developing Multicultural Student Projects

This chapter discusses procedures and resources which the instructor can use in formulating multicultural student projects.[1]

DEVELOPING THE PROJECT

Setting and Communicating Objectives

Instructors' objectives for student projects are generally similar to those for the course: mastering content; improving writing and thinking skills; and, in many cases, developing library research skills. Instructors often also harbor the hope that along the way students will experience the satisfaction that comes from discovering new ideas and will realize that sifting through information and organizing it into a coherent statement, although difficult and frequently frustrating, can, in the end, be a rewarding experience.

Although there may be three primary objectives—content, writing, and library research—not every assignment must include them all. If the concern is research and content, there is no need to require that the student write (and the instructor read!) long discussions of the results of student research; some projects require little or no writing. If the objectives are limited to writing and content or only to content, the information can be based on assigned or reserve reading and need not involve library research. However, it is important that students who are doing assignments based on reading materials in the reserve room should not be misled into thinking they are doing research.

No matter how simple or complex the objectives of the assignment, students need to understand what those objectives are and to recognize them as reasonable and important. Students who truly understand that diversity is an objective of the assignment are more likely to frame their questions and their research to incorporate diversity. Those who understand the relationship between clear thinking and clear writing and who are aware that both are among the objectives of the assignment are more likely to spend the extra time on organization, grammar, and rewriting. Similarly, students are less likely to begrudge the time needed for organized and effective research if they understand that learning library skills is one of the objectives of the assignment.

Structuring Assignments

Today most educators recognize that it is during the *process* of researching and writing that learning takes place. The final product is a report of that learning. There is also increasing recognition of the value of having the instructor participate in the process, a value which is increased when there is a multicultural objective for the assignment. Structuring assignments so that they are composed of a number of small interrelated projects done sequentially will enable the instructor to take part in the entire process, including providing guidance with any problems arising from the multicultural aspects of the assignment. In this way faculty interaction will not be limited to evaluating and grading the final result.

In addition to the opportunity for the instructor to participate in the process of learning which takes place during research and writing, structured assignments have other advantages:

- The multiple deadlines insure that all work will not be left to the end. They make it more likely that your assignment will be given appropriate amounts of time in a student's busy schedule.

- They permit early identification of problems so that those who need help in reading or writing can be referred to appropriate tutors early in the semester.

- They reinforce the importance of rewriting and editing. Students need to be told that everyone (including their instructor) needs to do several drafts. None of us would think of submitting a manuscript to a publisher without having it read several times by a friend or colleague; students have to show their drafts to us. (Peer review of an early draft by a classmate can also benefit both the student author and the student reviewer.)

- Faculty interaction during the process provides an opportunity to raise questions and to encourage or stimulate a broader, more diverse approach wherever it is appropriate.

Faculty sometimes fear that multiple deadlines will result in additional work for them. To say that this will definitely not be true would be simplistic; however, there are strategies that can minimize any additional load. The early phases need only be read and commented on but not graded. As noted above, some of the alternatives lend themselves to peer evaluation. Finally, the finished paper will be better as a result of your participation in the process, and, as faculty all know, it is much easier to grade a good paper than a poor one.

Below is a list of methods for structuring assignments; each may be used alone, or several may be combined.

Research worksheets. A research worksheet is a form on which students record (and report) the steps in their research process. Student researchers are asked to list the titles and years of the periodical indexes used (whether online, CD-ROM, or print), the subject headings consulted, key word and subject searches used in the catalog, and reference books consulted. Every step is recorded, whether or not it has proven fruitful! This is a way of giving students credit for taking appropriate steps even when they do not result in information which will be useful in the final project. Worksheets are also a way for the instructor to be sure from the start that the project is on track. Once students know the specifics that are required, they can devise their own worksheets or provide the information in journal or logbook format. Predesigned research worksheets are available in many college libraries. Some samples appear in Appendix A of this book.[2]

Preliminary bibliography. A familiar form used by many, a preliminary bibliography helps to insure that the sources used in the assignment will provide the full range of information needed. It is useful to ask that the potential sources be annotated and their relation to the topic be described to insure that the materials have been consulted and not just listed. When diversity is one of the objectives, students can be asked to comment on their selections in this context.

Written report on the first few items read. This is a more extensive project than the preliminary bibliography. The report can be a single paragraph or several pages. If experience in different modes of writing would be helpful, the assignment can specify that one item be summarized, a second be analyzed, and a third be outlined. This is a good project for peer evaluation by individuals or in small groups.

Preliminary outline. It is helpful if the preliminary outline contains brief descriptions of what will be included and which resources will be used in specific sections. This informal, written description will insure that students are beginning to think about the project's final shape, and it will show whether or not the reading has been integrated.

Note cards. The instructor can look through the student's note cards to insure that the project is going smoothly. It is useful to students (and to instructors) if students are directed to keep cards in two colors: one for summaries of the readings and the other for analysis, evaluations, reactions, and plans for final use. The two colors can also make it simpler to see if the student is thinking about the multicultural aspects of the assignment.

Preliminary draft. Regardless of whether any of the preceding suggestions are adopted, most instructors recognize that their active involvement with a preliminary draft is essential to the learning process. Since this is a point where the student can still benefit (i.e., learn something and not only get a better grade) from the instructor's comments, it is a natural place in the process to expend time. If students are required to return the preliminary draft with the final paper, reading that final paper will take correspondingly less time. One need only see the extent to which one's comments have been acted on, and not necessarily intensively reread the entire paper.

Providing a List of Topics

Some instructors hope to increase interest and motivation by giving students the freedom "to write about anything you want." Unfortunately, this approach really represents only the illusion of freedom. Undergraduates, particularly those in the lower division, may be limited in both experience and knowledge. The instructor is the expert in the field, the instructor has set the objectives for the assignment, and the instructor is best able to devise a research topic which will enable the student to meet those objectives. In addition, it is only by controlling the topics that the instructor can insure that students are able to approach their research within a multicultural context.

For these reasons, instructors are urged to provide students with a list of suggested topics for their projects (providing such a list does not mean that students who have their own ideas for topics should not pursue them). For many students, the choice of a topic is the most difficult part of a research assignment. Academic librarians, frequently consulted by students desperately seeking a topic, can attest to their distress. We see them devoting hours to making what may ultimately turn out to be a poor decision, because library resources are inadequate, the topic is too broad or too narrow, or the level of research needed is too complex. In all such cases, time is consumed in unproductive work, increasing the students' frustration without contributing to their knowledge or skills.

Even the most interesting topics, however, are interesting only if one knows something about them. Thus, consider briefly annotating the topics on your list. The annotation is a good way to reinforce a request for a multicultural approach. Making the annotations enticing (like the "coming attractions" in the movies) can stimulate interest and an enthusiastic start for the project.

Instructors in subject disciplines who are attempting to incorporate a more diverse approach will probably have no difficulty devising appropriate lists of topics for student research. However, they, as well as instructors in skills courses, might find the next section of this chapter helpful. It discusses generic topics useful in constructing research projects which can easily encompass diversity objectives.

GENERIC TOPICS FOR DIVERSITY-RELATED STUDENT RESEARCH

Throughout this section the reader will find references to Chapter 6. That chapter contains substantial annotations to resources which will be useful to instructors who choose to design the kinds of projects described below, and to students who want to undertake those projects.

Biographies

To embrace the concept of multiculturalism, we need to become listeners; we need not only to look at people from the outside, but to hear people in their own voices. Among the best ways to do this is to read and write biographies and autobiographies.

The basic pattern of a life is familiar no matter how unusual the details, which is one reason students frequently do well with biographical assignments. They are accustomed to thinking about people; indeed, if there is one area in which they have had experience looking for hidden meanings, analyzing and comparing statements, and looking for causes and effects, it is the realm of human behavior. Well-known people of every ethnicity and race—or those who should be well known—can be studied for their contributions. Little-known or unknown people, including the working-class people so often overlooked, can be studied for their ability to illuminate a way of life, a class of people, an occupation, an event, or a movement.

There are numerous bibliographic tools which can be used to select subjects for biographical study. Both general and specialized biographical directories and bibliographies of biographies contain indexes which allow one to locate members of specific occupational, ethnic, or religious groups, women, people with disabilities, and residents of specific places. A number of these directories include the not-so-famous and the anonymous as well as the famous.

Thanks to today's highly developed bibliographic tools even undergraduates can now have access to some of the primary sources of biographical study: the autobiographies, letters, and journals on which those studies are based. These sources are available not only for information about the powerful and famous, but also for large numbers of people previously overlooked by traditional historians. Sources such as Brumble's *An Annotated Bibliography of American Indian and Eskimo Autobiographies*, Brignano's *Black Americans in Autobiography*, and Siegel and Finley's *Women in the Scientific Search: An American Biobibliography, 1724–1979* are only a few examples of the bibliographies available. See the section "Biographical Directories" in Chapter 6 for a discussion of relevant biographical dictionaries and directories.

Associations

Associations are instructive and interesting topics for research. Students are as familiar with the concept of groups of people who join together for a specific purpose as they are with the pattern of individual lives. In addition, associations as research topics are relatively easy to limit in scope.

Studying associations is a particularly good way to come to know women and minority groups. From the earliest days of the Republic, residents of this country who possessed little or no power (as well as those in power) have attempted to help themselves and others through guilds, clubs, fraternal groups, labor unions, societies, and many other kinds of associations. It is in these associations, that one can see nineteenth- and early twentieth-century women—white and black—displaying managerial, political, organizational, and financial skills, as well as good intentions and hard work. The histories of these groups easily refute the assertions that women did not have leadership or managerial skills or that

African Americans did not have the ability to organize independently. The voices and concerns of workers of many ethnicities can also be heard by studying the early workingmen's associations and the labor unions which evolved from them. Finally, organized attempts by the oppressed to improve their own conditions can be traced through a study of the civil rights associations.

The scope of possible topics related to associations is broad. It can encompass full-scale studies of associations such as the New York Female Moral Reform Society, founded in 1830, or the National Association of Colored Womens Clubs, founded in 1896, or the League of United Latin-American Citizens (LULAC), founded in Texas in 1929. Research topics can also include more modest studies, such as an interview with a member of the faculty who belongs to the Association for Women in Mathematics, or a librarian who participates in the Black Caucus of the American Library Association, or a member of the National Organization of Black Law Enforcement Executives (NOBLE).

Both instructor and student will find Anne Firor Scott's *Natural Allies: Women's Associations in American History* a fascinating introduction to this subject. Lists of minority associations can be found in the appropriate chapters in James A. Banks's *Teaching Strategies for Ethnic Studies*[3] and in the sources discussed in the section "Directories" in Chapter 6. Books about associations concerned with specific subjects or ethnic groups can be found in the library's online catalog by using the word SOCIETIES in a key word search.

Specific Groups

Racial, Ethnic, and Religious Groups. When selecting this option for student research, one is faced with a familiar choice. Students may be told either to "write about any group which interests you," which in almost all instances will be a group with which the student already identifies, or to "select from this list a group to which you do not belong." The advantages of choosing a familiar group are well known: an already existing interest, psychological reinforcement and self-identity, and positive role models with whom to identify. The advantages of choosing an unfamiliar group, however, are less often enumerated. They include the opportunity to learn about a new group and to compare the new group with the known group, possible development of empathy for a group previously ignored, and a general broadening of one's perspective on the world. Above all, research into an unfamiliar ethnic group provides an opportunity to confront one's own ethnocentricity and limited worldview. In the author's admittedly limited experience, few persons among even the most diversity-concerned academics and students in New York City devote much thought to Native Americans when they are discussing problems of minority groups. Similarly, people in California don't automatically think about the difficulties faced by nineteenth-century immigrants from Ireland.

Because the advantages of each choice are so different, students who research an ethnic group which is basically unfamiliar to them will have a very different experience from those whose research is largely concentrated on groups with which they are familiar.

Students attempting to narrow the focus of their research on a specific ethnic, religious, or racial group might look at one or more of the following: impact of modernization, ties to homeland, attitudes toward homeland, internal divisions, conflict with other groups, role of education, strategies adopted to maintain language and religion, and acculturation.[4] The concentration might also be on women, on children and childhood, on adolescence, or on a specific time period.

Students looking for an overview of an unfamiliar group might consult the *Harvard Encyclopedia of American Ethnic Groups,* which includes essays on 106 specific groups, or the ten-volume *Encyclopedia of World Cultures,* which includes articles on 1,500 groups. Both are discussed more fully in Chapter 6 in the section "Encyclopedias and Other Overviews."

Women. Topics can be developed which concentrate specifically on the role or condition of women among the majority white population, any minority population, or in a country other than our own. The topic can be narrowed by limiting the time frame or by focusing on specific professions, occupations, or life stages.

Other Countries. Knowledge of other countries is vital to a comprehensive worldview. Any topic can automatically be broadened in its outlook by focusing on events, ideas, and people in other countries.

Economic Classes. Most of what is discussed in college classrooms is information from and about the middle class or the upper class. Student research projects can be designed to focus on an event; a time period; or a literary, educational, or social movement from the point of view of the working class, the poor, or the unemployed.

Specific Events

Specific events which occur within a limited time period, particularly those of a spectacular nature, make good research topics for lower-division students. Events such as the Detroit race riots of 1943 or 1967, the Triangle shirt-waist factory fire in New York City in 1911, the anti-Chinese riot in Rock Springs, Wyoming, in 1885, and the homestead strike of 1892 appear to be endlessly fascinating to students (many of whom feel that protest and violence never occurred before their lifetime). Such events offer the opportunity to study minority and majority, the powerful and the powerless.[5] Any specific event can be studied from the point of view of those who were participants, those who were uninvolved, and those in positions of power.

PRIMARY SOURCES FOR DIVERSITY-RELATED STUDENT RESEARCH

Advantages of Using Primary Sources

Until recently, the most exciting aspect of library research—the gleaning and processing of information from primary sources—was limited to "serious" scholars because of the rarity and location of the documents. Today, microforms, reprint publishers, CD-ROM full-text databases, and video archives have made research in primary sources possible for all, including undergraduates. Widespread interest in multicultural research, particularly African American studies and women studies, has insured that a fairly substantial number of sources will reflect those interests. It is the rare library which does not have at least a few primary sources in microform. Since cataloging of this type of material is often either nonexistent or too general to be helpful to the average reader, it is wise to discuss with a librarian your desire to use primary sources. In many cases, materials bought for a highly specialized course can be adapted for use in other courses.

There are three good reasons to make primary sources the basis of student research assignments.

- Students enjoy them. Evidence from librarians and instructors makes clear that students enjoy the challenge of going directly to original sources to reconstruct the life, attitudes, and events of an earlier period. For students who have previously experienced boredom or failure with research projects, using primary sources can put research into a new perspective.

- An understanding of the nature of primary sources is basic to an understanding of scholarly research methods. As Thomas C. Holt has written:

  The biases that left slaves, as people, out of the history of slavery were not simply racial. They more often had to do with what could be considered legitimate and illegitimate sources. This in turn had to do with how knowledge, or fact itself, was defined. . . . The reason Afro-Americans were so long excluded is not because they had no history, an impossibility where life and experience exists; . . . nor that there were no sources from which to write the history—clearly there were and are. . . . Rather it was that these sources remained unseen.[6]

- Finally, and most important for increasing student understanding of diversity, primary sources are an extremely effective way to stimulate a critical approach to reading and thinking. By reading this type of material, students learn to look for hidden assumptions, and variant meanings of words, and to recognize that what is unsaid can be as important as what is said. This type of research, where the way in which material is read can be more important than the amount read, emphasizes that thinking, rather than reading, is the essence of research.[7]

Primary sources can be an effective educational tool in a wide variety of courses. They enable students to experience, in as direct a way as possible, the life of another person, events in another era, or the ambience of another place. Reading the actual words of the Chinese Exclusion Act, hearing the words (and seeing the pictures) of Holocaust survivors, reading a slave's diary, all carry an impact far beyond merely reading about these people and events.

The primary sources most readily available are on microfilm or microfiche. Instructors who shudder at the memory of sitting in a basement room and taking endless notes while burying their heads and shoulders in an old-fashioned microfilm reader should know that the equipment has improved. Although microfilm is still not an unalloyed joy to use, it is now possible to read it in a normally lit room and to make good-quality, plain-paper copies. Libraries which have not adapted to these changes should be strongly urged to do so.

Microfiche has several advantages over microfilm. Portable microfiche readers, although not capable of making copies, enable the researcher to use the fiche anywhere. More important, many portable readers are capable of displaying the images on a wall or screen, and they can thus become a useful tool in the classroom.[8]

Widely Available Primary Sources

Magazines and Newspapers. These represent primary sources in their simplest and most widely available form. Formats with which students are thoroughly familiar, articles in newspapers and magazines are fairly short, easy to understand, and in many cases have even been indexed for researchers. Looking at popular magazines and newspapers from an earlier period is an excellent way to alert students to the manner in which unstated messages can be conveyed. The very unfamiliarity of appearance of periodicals and newspapers from fifty or a hundred years ago tends to focus attention. Students looking for attitudes toward minorities, toward women, or toward immigrants in the articles, the advertising, the photographs, or the drawings in these sources will learn something about the attitudes of an earlier period. In the process, they might also learn to look at contemporary media more critically.

Students can browse through several years' worth of a particular journal, look at five or ten different journals published in the same year, or look for information on a particular subject by using the indexes which are available to some of these journals. Among the thousands of possible topics are a comparison of Native American periodicals with some of the popular magazines (including *Overland Monthly, Harpers Weekly,* and *Leslie's Illustrated*) which gave Americans their picture of Indians and the West in the late nineteenth and early twentieth century; discussions of bilingual education in ethnic magazines of the same period; or the reporting of slave revolts in *Friends' Review* (a Quaker publication which started in 1848) and in the *New York Times.*

In addition to the *New York Times,* which began publication in 1851, there are hundreds of periodicals available in microform, including *The Anti-Slavery Record* (1835–1838); the *Indian School Record* (1902–1952) and *The Native American* (1900–1931); and *The Negro Music Journal* (1902–1903); and the *Lowell Offering,* the magazine written by the "shop-girls" of Lowell, Massachusetts, from 1840 to 1845. Directories of nineteenth- and early twentieth-century journals, as well as information about obtaining these journals and about guides and indexes to their contents, are found in the section "Selected Primary Sources: Newspapers and Magazines of the Nineteenth and Early Twentieth Centures" in Chapter 6.

Archives in Microform. Most college libraries own at least a few primary sources on microfilm which were purchased for the use of graduate students or faculty. Among those which could be most suitably used for undergraduate multicultural research topics are the *Tuskegee Institute News Clipping File* and the *Jane Addams Papers*. These and others are described in Chapter 6 in the section "Selected Primary Sources: Documents, Archives, and Research Collections."

Books as Primary Sources. Primary sources need not be archival or in microform. Remember that yesterday's ideas are today's history, and consider an assignment based on monographs and reference books published in an earlier period. Many of these are now available in reprint series, and older colleges may have original printings still in their stacks. (Be aware, however, that many large libraries do not provide information about their older materials in the online catalog; it is best to ask the librarian.)

James Francis Brown's *Our Racial and National Minorities: Their History, Contributions, and Present Problems*, first published in 1937, would be a useful volume in this regard.[9] A genuine precursor to the *Harvard Encyclopedia of American Ethnic Groups*, Brown's book includes essays on topics related to minorities, immigration, and prejudice, as well as articles on the press, schools, language, and crime. The articles devoted to individual ethnic groups discuss immigration history, assimilation, current problems, and contributions to American life. A serious and scholarly work, whose contributors include James Weldon Johnson and Harry Schneiderman, Brown's book contains an extensive general bibliography plus separate bibliographies for each group treated. These bibliographies are good sources for monographs published early in the century.

Visual Sources. Today's intensely visual generation might welcome and benefit from research projects based on the analysis of visual sources. Posters, photographs, and cartoons can be valuable as primary sources which carry subtle as well as overt messages. They are rich sources for reflecting popular as well as official viewpoints and are thus valuable for reflecting attitudes toward minorities, immigrants, "foreigners," and working people. Learning to analyze them for both subtle and overt messages, and for hidden (and not so hidden) prejudices and biases, can be interesting as a research project and useful in everyday life. The section "Visual Sources" in Chapter 6 includes descriptions of a number of such sources.

Legal Sources. Legal decisions and briefs are a rich but frequently overlooked category of primary sources. The deliberations and decisions of the United States Supreme Court have played a major role in shaping immigration policies, race relations, and minority rights throughout our history.

The *United States Reports*, containing decisions of the Supreme Court from 1754 on, should be available in the library of almost every college offering a bachelor's degree. These are the classic-looking law books; they are what you see behind Perry Mason's desk on TV. With a bit of orientation and some help from a legal dictionary, most students can cope intelligently with those decisions which pertain to political or social issues. Students generally react very positively to the use of this material because of its obvious relevance to the "real world."

Less widely available, but certainly in every law school library, is *Landmark Briefs and Arguments of the Supreme Court of the United States*.[10] This set, available on microfiche or in hard copy, contains the legal briefs, the supporting documents, and the oral arguments for each case decided by the Supreme Court. Reading the actual lawyers' briefs, and especially hearing the questions and answers during the oral presentations, can involve and enlighten many formerly "uninterested" students.

Although many court decisions are well known, others, not so familiar, are also relevant. While legal research tools can help isolate cases on particular topics (ask the librarian for help with these), many instructors will find their purposes well served by *Historic U.S. Court Cases, 1690–1990: An Encyclopedia*, edited by John W. Johnson.[11] This volume summarizes and comments on important cases and attempts to place each one in its historic context. Each case is discussed separately, and full citations and a bibliography are provided. Thirty cases are discussed in the section devoted to "Race and Gender in American Law."

WORKING WITH THE LIBRARY

Instructors interested in expanding the diversity of their courses might benefit from consulting a librarian. Librarians are adept at locating sources to provide a fast overview or orientation to a subject, as well as locating sources for more detailed information. If the library in your institution does not have an appropriate collection to support either faculty's needs for self-education in areas related to diversity or students' research needs in those areas, the library administration should be pressed to expand the acquisitions policies. In addition to all the more obvious reasons for doing so, it could be pointed out that the ability of a library to support multicultural research is frequently assessed during accreditation visits.

It is strongly recommended that the instructor consult the library staff before assigning new research projects to students. This is even more vital if the assignment is somewhat unusual. Such prior consultation can insure that the materials needed to successfully complete the assignment are available and that librarians, aware of your objectives, can support them.

Many of the research projects discussed in this book require an ability to use the library efficiently. Instructors who question their students' ability to do so should arrange for the library to provide instruction in research processes for the class. Even those students who have had considerable experience using the library can undoubtedly learn about additional resources and more sophisticated searching techniques. Because of the interdisciplinary nature of research related to ethnicity and diversity, such instruction is especially important. Most libraries provide library instruction services; if yours does not, talk to the library director or the provost about introducing them. Most regional accrediting associations now require that libraries provide formal instruction in research methods for students on all levels.

NOTES

1. The material in this section is applicable to student research and writing assignments in all subjects whether or not there is a diversity component. Readers desiring a fuller discussion of some of these topics should consult the author's previous book, *Research Projects for College Students: What to Write Across the Curriculum* (New York: Greenwood, 1988).

2. Additional samples are reproduced in *Research Projects for College Students*. The librarian in your institution can contact LOEX (National Library Orientation Exchange) at the University Library, Eastern Michigan University, Ypsilanti, MI, 48197, for more examples.

3. James A. Banks, *Teaching Strategies for Ethnic Studies*, 5th ed. (Boston: Allyn and Bacon, 1991).

4. This suggested list of topics is adapted from John D. Buenker and Lorman A. Ratner, eds., *Multiculturalism in the United States: A Comparative Guide to Acculturation and Ethnicity* (New York: Greenwood, 1992).

5. Banks, *Teaching Strategies for Ethnic Studies,* is a particularly good one-volume source of specific events of this type.

6. Thomas C. Holt, "Introduction: Whither Now and Why?" in Darlene Clark Hine, ed., *The State of Afro-American History: Past, Present, and Future* (Baton Rouge: Louisiana State University Press, 1986), p. 6.

7. For descriptions of the use of primary sources with undergraduates, see T. H. Breen, "Keeping Pace with the Past: Puritans and Planters among the Microforms," *Microform Review* 20 (1991): 57–60; and Shirla R. McClain and Ambrose A. Clegg, Jr., "Words, Records, and Beyond: Studying about Local Ethnic Groups Through Primary Sources," *Social Education* 41 (1977): 382–388.

8. Pat Flowers, "Reference Applications of Color Microfiche: The World in the Palm of Your Hand," *Microform Review* 21 (spring 1992): 65, n. 7, is a brief discussion of portable microfiche readers.

9. James Francis Brown, ed., *Our Racial and National Minorities: Their History, Contributions, and Present Problems* (New York: Prentice Hall, 1937). A revised edition, edited by Brown and Joseph S. Roucek, was given the title *One America: The History,*

Contributions, and Present Problems of Our Racial and National Minorities, published in 1945 by Prentice Hall, and reprinted in 1970 by the Negro Universities Press.

10. *Landmark Briefs and Arguments of the Supreme Court of the United States* (Frederick, MD: University Publications of America, 1978–).

11. John W. Johnson, *Historic U.S. Court Cases, 1690–1990: An Encyclopedia* (New York: Garland, 1992).

4

Student Projects:
The Diversity Perspective

This chapter describes student projects which can be used to enhance the diversity content of courses in all disciplines. Some of the projects discussed require library research; others do not. Included are suggestions which offer opportunities to present information orally or in writing, and to work individually or in groups. Most projects are extremely flexible in terms of the amount of work required.

LIBRARY RESEARCH ASSIGNMENTS: TERM PAPERS AND THEIR ALTERNATIVES

Students customarily organize and present information obtained from research by writing term papers. The advantages of term papers are that students are familiar with them and they can range greatly in size. However, their very familiarity means that traditional term papers rarely generate a sense of excitement in students. Thus, alternatives are described below.

All the alternative formats for presenting research discussed in this chapter have been selected because of their usefulness in incorporating diversity objectives. In order to make them practical in as many contexts as possible, they are also adaptable in terms of the amount of time required of students and of instructors. Some require a good deal of imagination. Many may ignite a spark of real enthusiasm in students tired of more traditional assignments or discouraged about their ability to produce work in the traditional format. All are almost certain guarantees against plagiarism.

Anthologies

Anthologies can be an extremely flexible method of presenting research. Ask students to

- Locate and read a specific number of articles on their chosen topic.
- Photocopy the articles and assemble them in a folder.
- Write a general introduction which demonstrates an overall understanding of the subject.
- Write brief introductions for each item, describing it and explaining why it was included and how it relates to the anthology as a whole.

The assignment can be made more challenging and interesting if you request that it include some kind of visual material: portraits, photographs, reproductions of paintings or buildings, maps, cartoons, or posters.

Multicultural topics can be the basis of this assignment, or traditional topics can be used with the request that minorities and women be represented among the authors. In researching some topics, students may have difficulty locating work by such authors; this difficulty can lead to useful class discussions.

The advantages of the anthology are

- It is a format which is usually familiar to students. If it is not, it can be easily demonstrated.
- It is flexible. It can require twelve articles, three illustrations, and a ten-page introduction, or be limited to five articles and a two-page introduction.
- It can enable students to practice a variety of library research procedures.
- It results in a unique product that students can feel pride in having created.
- It can be relatively quick and easy for the instructor to grade.
- It is easily adapted as a group project.

Sourcebooks

A variation on the anthology format, sourcebooks require students to locate and reproduce primary sources. Newspaper and magazine articles, excerpts from diaries, speeches, songs, government reports, relevant cases, statutes, and administrative regulations are among the endless examples of items appropriate for a sourcebook. Because of the many types of materials which are appropriate, sourcebooks are particularly useful for learning a variety of library research skills.

A sourcebook on the Japanese internment camps of World War II could include excerpts from the law establishing the camps, copies of newspaper articles describing the camps, excerpts from contemporary letters and diaries of those interned and later reminiscences by them and their families, editorial reaction to the camps from a variety of newspapers, photographs of the camps and the people in them, and excerpts from the case law surrounding the issue. A sourcebook on the building of the U.S. railroad system in the nineteenth century could include contemporary illustrations of the work being done, letters from Chinese workers, reminiscences of Irish workers, descriptions by Native Americans, newspaper stories, old maps, cartoons, and folk songs.

Students compiling sourcebooks on multicultural topics will be able to go beyond the summaries and distillations of textbooks and see the official language and/or the contemporary popular language used. In addition, as discussed in the previous chapter, use of primary sources can introduce students to the type of critical reading essential to an understanding of subtle biases, unspoken generalizations, and unquestioned norms.

Role-Playing

Although role-playing is an in-class activity, it is included in this section on library research projects because it can be based on such research. In many cases, however, it can be just as effectively done based on assigned readings and class discussions. A multitude of role-playing activities can be adapted to introduce or highlight multicultural information and approaches or to present alternative points of view. Five-minute role-plays based on common knowledge or information from assigned readings can be introduced into an established syllabus without adding to the amount of outside work required of students or the instructor. Other role-playing projects that require more student research might be considered as alternatives to the traditional research paper assignment.

There are several conditions necessary for this kind of activity to be truly useful:

- The instructor should have a clear idea of the objective of the activity.
- Students should understand the objective and view the activity as integral to the learning situation, not as an isolated activity.

- The classroom environment should be open and nonthreatening.
- Students should not be graded on their role-playing (although they may be graded on the information it contains).
- Strict time limits should be imposed (five to ten minutes are often enough).
- The role-playing situation should be used as the basis of class discussion.[1]

Conversations and Case Studies. These are the simplest and most common form of role-playing. We know that much of what happens during speech communication (such as eye contact, who speaks to whom, forms of address, body language, and topics) is culturally and historically determined. Role-playing conversations can make students more aware of these determinants.

In structuring a conversation or case study, define a situation which is relevant to students and which does not have a clear "yes" or "no" solution. Ask students to volunteer for roles. One instructor describes a class on treating the delinquent adolescent which discusses drug abuse. A situation is set up in which the members of the family are called to jail after being notified that the adolescent has been picked up for drug possession. The characters are the family, the adolescent, and the police officer. Not only can the situation be made relevant to the class, but it can also be used to illustrate problems of real or perceived discrimination if the specifics of the situation are manipulated. The nature of the family, the gender of the offender and of the police officer, the ethnicity, race, and social class of the participants, and the prior history of the adolescent can all be varied.[2] Two groups can present the same role-play, changing one or more variables, such as race, gender, or occupation. A lively class discussion is likely to follow.

In other subject areas, the class can be challenged to have a conversation as if they were people from another culture or another time. Students in a nineteenth-century British literature class can become characters from Victorian London; those in a class on U.S. history can become Native Americans forced out of their traditional homelands, shopgirls in the Lowell factories, or Chinese laborers working on the railroad.

An interesting ongoing role-play is described by Meyers and Jones. In a course on eighteenth-century Europe, students are asked to create a character of specific gender, religion, class, and occupation born in France between 1770 and 1780 and write a description of that person including personality and role in society. Periodically during the semester, the instructor asks students to describe their characters' actions or reactions to events. Meyers and Jones note that "students are consciously and continually analyzing the effect of a historical event on specific individuals and the impact of those individuals on events."[3]

Certain disciplines lend themselves to case-study types of role-playing. Thus, in a nursing or social work class, one student can be the client and another the professional during an intake interview, with one or the other character being African American, non-English-speaking, or elderly. In a business administration class, a male supervisor can be interviewing a female potential employee (or vice versa); or negotiations for a contract can be taking place between an American business executive and a Japanese counterpart. The possibilities are endless. It might be interesting to videotape these interactions for class discussion.

Role-Playing from Fiction. After reading a novel, students can choose a character whom they would be willing to portray. This format can become a group project in which students who choose the same character work together and collectively answer questions directed to that character by the class. Individual students can also be asked to create a conversation among the characters on a specified topic. For example, characters in *The Great Gatsby* can reflect on the lives of their servants, those in Cooper's *The Deerslayer* or *The Last of the Mohicans* could talk about their perceptions of Indians, or those in Twain's *Adventures of Huckleberry Finn* might give their views of Huck's difficult decision not to betray his Black friend Jim.

Get into the Act. Many instructors are frustrated actors or actresses. Consider role-playing yourself and adopt another persona for a class session: Frederick Douglass or Chief Joseph of the Nez Perce lecturing to an American history class, or Madame Curie lecturing to a chemistry class. You could also invent your own character: a Chinese immigrant to California in 1840, or a member of the Sons of the Golden West, an organization deeply opposed to Chinese immigration; or a woman who wants to study medicine in 1880, or the head of the medical school which refused to admit her. Dressing for the occasion can lend additional panache to the presentation. Tell the class ahead of time about the expected honored guest and instruct them that they must come prepared to ask relevant (and even embarrassing!) questions.

Structured Dialogues

Imaginary conversations between historical characters can be presented either orally or in writing; the oral presentation format presents a nice opportunity for small-group work. The true value of such a dialogue is the level of understanding and integration of information which it stimulates. Dialogues require students to recast ideas and information into their own personal way of speaking (different from a paraphrase or a summary). Students cannot "bluff" an understanding if they need to explain and defend ideas in a dialogue.[4]

Among the dialogues which might be used are: Niccolò Machiavelli and Lao-Tzu discussing their political viewpoints; Martin Luther King, Jr., and Henry David Thoreau discussing civil disobedience; Isaac Newton and Albert Einstein discussing God; Karl Marx and John Kenneth Galbraith discussing poverty; and Euclid and Karl Gauss on whether parallel lines can meet. One could restage the great debate at Valladolid, Spain, in 1550 when Bartolomé de Las Casas and Jan Gines de Sepulveda debated whether Indians "were men or monkeys, whether they were mere brutes or were capable of rational thought, and whether or not God intended them to be permanent slaves of their European overlords."[5]

Panel Discussions

A group of students could read articles representing different viewpoints on the same topic, and then present a panel discussion. For instructors who like to stimulate group work, the class can be divided into four or five groups. Everyone in each group will read the same article, discuss it, and select a representative to present the group's perceptions of the highlights of the article. During the panel discussion, the rest of the class should take notes and formulate questions with which to challenge the panel. As the discussion develops, panel members may call on "advisors" from their group to answer some questions.

Letters

Letters are an alternative way to communicate information. By their nature they provide a defined audience and are an inherently flexible form. They can be short or long, formal or very informal, require descriptive writing or necessitate more expressive language. Short, informal letters lend themselves well to peer evaluation. The assignment can be a single letter or a series of letters written over the semester.

The letters can be addressed by the student to a real person or a fictitious one, and either a person now living or from some other time in history. A good way to force recognition of basic assumptions and prior knowledge to the forefront is to address a letter explaining a class discussion or required reading to a person in another country. The letters can also be written as if the author were someone else—either real, symbolic, or from fiction. All those people described above as participants in role-plays or dialogues can be letter writers if a written rather than an oral assignment is preferred.

Time-Lines

If the instructor has not provided a time-line for the class (see Chapter 2), constructing one could be an interesting project for students working either as individuals or in groups. Time-lines can include political events; births, deaths, and accomplishments of well-known people; literature, art, and music; daily life; scientific and historical discoveries; inventions; and so on. If the assignment requires that specific ethnic groups, economic classes, countries, or regions be included, then the time-line will of necessity become an exercise in multiculturalism.

This project is particularly useful when the instructor desires to give a clearly defined research assignment, but does not want to increase the amount of writing being required of students.

Exhibitions

Designing exhibitions is another way of saying "Explain this" and asking students to demonstrate how they would best present that explanation to a specific audience. It is like planning a multimedia term paper.[6]

Students in almost any subject area can be asked to design (in theory) an exhibition for a museum or gallery. The project, which would be good for group work, could involve

- Deciding on the topic.
- Deciding on the materials to be displayed, remembering that museum displays can include a broad range of actual objects as well as pictures and illustrations.
- Explaining why the particular items were chosen.
- Writing introductory materials for the entrance wall of the exhibit or for an exhibit brochure.
- Writing labels for each item to explain it to visitors.
- Writing publicity releases.

The exhibit can be designed to appeal to children or adults. It could be for a major museum with diverse visitors or a smaller establishment that would appeal to a specific ethnic or religious audience or to groups from specific neighborhoods. The exhibit could even be designed for a small "wall gallery" in a rehabilitation center, factory, senior residence, welfare shelter, or college cafeteria.

Although one tends to think of projects like this in terms of art history, exhibits can be designed to illustrate a broad range of topics related to diversity. A few random examples: mathematical principles of the Aztec Indians; effects of economic development in Papua New Guinea; significant contributions by women physicists; living conditions of workers in Victorian London; Native Americans prior to Columbus; popular music in India; individual or group biographies; and the history of anything ranging from China or Egypt to modern dance or the electric kitchen stove.

Exhibition projects which do not have a multicultural subject can still be used to heighten sensitivity to multiculturalism by varying the audience for which they are designed.

Research Proposals

Even undergraduates understand the role which funded research plays in today's world. Since we know that a substantial amount of grant money is now allocated to projects related in some way to diversity, writing a grant proposal is a realistic way to introduce students to this kind of thinking.

Since grant funding is of particular importance in science and mathematics, writing proposals related to diversity is a particularly appropriate way to introduce writing into those classes and to focus students' attention on issues of multiculturalism within those disciplines. Student proposals might focus on issues like programs to attract women and minorities into physics, ways to alleviate "math anxiety," or correctives to the exclusive use of male subjects in medical experiments. Whatever the topic, the research proposal should follow standard formats and explain why the idea is important, outline the methodology, and include a review of previous research in the area.

Newspaper Articles or Complete Newspapers

Student research on any topic can be presented in the form of a newspaper article or, depending on the amount of analysis and opinion desired, as a feature column or an editorial. The research process and topics are the same as for a traditional term paper, but the formal academic documentation which so often intimidates students would not be required. (However, sources of information and ideas can be described in an informal note to the instructor.)

Where research topics are centered around a single theme, a group of students or a small class can be challenged to produce an entire newspaper including articles, features, editorials, illustrations, letters to the editor, interviews, and cartoons. Students in a class on slavery and abolitionism can produce a Quaker newspaper from the 1850s. One group of students in a class on the Industrial Revolution can produce a newspaper written by union organizers, while another group can write one by the manufacturers. An art history class can attempt an early twentieth-century *Women in Art* journal that explores issues of women's access to life-drawing classes and to exhibition space, and the lack of attention to women's traditional art forms such as embroidery, basketry, and weaving. Such projects require planning, but they present the opportunity to explore a broad array of issues related to diversity and also offer the possibility of using a variety of writing styles. In addition, they might prove to be a catalyst for reluctant researchers.

News Broadcasts for Radio or Television

This activity can be based on library research or on class discussions and required readings. The assignment is to decide what gets put into the broadcast and what gets left out, and to explain why. How would a newscast on a public station differ from that on a commercial station? Who will be interviewed? If it is a video, what visuals will be included? The topic of the newscast can be contemporary or historical. Students can be challenged to do an entire fifteen-minute show or to produce just a three-minute segment.

MULTICULTURAL PROJECTS WHICH DO NOT REQUIRE LIBRARY RESEARCH

As indicated earlier, several of the formats discussed in the section on library research projects can also be done based only on required readings and/or class discussions.

Reading for Multiculturalism

Once the class has been made aware of the instructor's concern for diversity issues—globalism, ethnicity, race, gender, age, sexual orientation, class, and so forth—students can be asked to look at all assigned readings through a multicultural prism. They can be told that they are expected to ask themselves the following kinds of questions about the material being read:

- Who is included? Who has been left out?
- Is there an unspoken bias in the text?
- Is there an unspoken bias in the illustrations?
- Whose point of view is reflected?
- How inclusive are the sources on which the reading is based?
- Is there inappropriate language?
- Are comparisons balanced? Is a typical person of one group compared only with an atypical person from another group?
- Are there subtle stereotypes?
- Is there a Eurocentric point of view? An Afrocentric point of view? Is it appropriate?
- Is there a place where the text could have been enriched by including more diverse viewpoints or information about other groups?
- Would a poor person, an older person, a person living in Australia or France, or a person of the opposite sex, another race, or a different sexual orientation have the same reaction to the reading which you do?

Being alert to questions such as these while doing assigned readings, and being asked to bring examples to the attention of the class, should result in a more thoughtful approach to the text. Extra credit can be offered for written responses.

If surveys or research studies are used at any point in the course, students can be asked to analyze them in terms of diversity: Is there bias in the questions? In the interpretations? Are any relevant groups left out? Can one make universal generalizations based on the subjects of the survey? Is the manner in which groups have been aggregated consistent? The large number of psychological surveys done with college students as the only population, generalizations about the entire population based on male-only medical research, and public opinion polls taken at specific subway exits are only a few of the kinds of situations which could be questioned.

Similarly, students can be encouraged to apply their multicultural prism to statistical tables in textbooks, in newspapers, and in campus publications. Can the numbers be read in any other way? Are aggregates used consistently, or are all Hispanics lumped together while Europeans are presented separately?

Rewrites

One way to help students achieve a higher level of comprehension about other groups and other periods is to give a rewrite assignment. Since such an assignment can be quite brief, students could work on it in small groups in class, as well as individually. A few examples of rewrite assignments:

- Rewrite these two pages of the textbook as they might have been written by a Native American, a person in China, or a homeless person. For example, the textbook statement "Alone in the wilderness, the frontier family had to protect itself from wild animals and unfriendly Indians" could be rewritten as "While the people were trying to live, farm, and hunt peacefully in their homelands, they had to constantly be on guard against marauding and invading whites."[7]

- Rewrite the table of contents of the textbook to better reflect the interests of a Chicano, a waiter or taxicab driver, or an older person.

- Develop an outline for a new chapter in the textbook which relates a group to which you belong (race, religion, gender, age, or nationality) to the topic.

- Rewrite a mainstream newspaper editorial on prison sentencing from the viewpoint of an incarcerated African American male or an article on welfare reform from the viewpoint of an elderly woman living on Social Security.

Guided Fantasies

Ask students to reflect on some aspect of the course as if they were of a different race, gender, age, or sexual orientation. This assignment could be strictly a homework exercise to stimulate thinking, or some of the responses could be read out loud (with students' permission) as the basis of a class discussion.[8]

For a more elaborate two-part exercise, the instructor might ask the students first to write an essay describing themselves—their race, class, age, religion, sexual orientation, and marital status—and how those characteristics affect their lives today and will affect their futures. As the second part, students choose an identity which is unlike their own in at least three areas and again describe how those characteristics affect their lives today and can be expected to affect their future.[9]

Guided Tours

Less personal but perhaps equally thought-provoking is the concept of providing a guided tour. Ask students to think about their city, their campus, or their home neighborhood. How would they describe it to a student from another country or from another part of our country, to a foreign political leader, or to a person who is a member of an ethnic or religious minority on campus or in the community? What physical features would they point out? Which local leaders would they talk about? How would they describe the social dynamics of the neighborhood? What would they say about the kinds of things available in the supermarket, the drug store, the local video store, or the public library branch?

The guided tour is a good way to get people to think about the most familiar things in their lives and to question basic assumptions. It is an assignment which, in addition to being obviously useful in skills courses and urban planning, could be adapted for use in courses in government, sociology, marketing, history, and education. The tour can be written in the form of a letter, an essay, a travel article, or a guidebook.[10] As with rewrite assignments, students can create these guided tours either individually or with one or more classmates. Even when the final written product is done individually, brainstorming the raw materials could be a team project.

Journals

To encourage students to reflect both on what they have been taught and what they have learned, an increasing number of instructors ask their students to keep a journal. Requesting that students keep a "diversity journal" is one way of focusing attention on issues of diversity without infringing on class time. Requirements can specify that entries be made weekly or biweekly, that entries be reflections on material read or discussed in class or include reactions to readings for other classes, or that entries reflect on events in the news, on campus, or on personal experiences. Journals can be required but not graded, or be offered as an extra-credit assignment. Requiring a diversity journal is one way to encourage students to approach all their reading with a view to evaluating the extent to which each book or article accurately reflects an appropriately inclusive worldview.

Media Content Analysis

If the subject of a course makes an analysis of media content relevant, students can analyze a single television show, an evening of sitcoms (or of commercials!), a week's worth of newspapers, or several issues of a specific popular magazine for examples of bias or stereotypes. Providing a worksheet or a checklist of things to look for can give structure and focus to the assignments. Among the areas which can be considered are population (How many African Americans, women, people with disabilities, or older people are represented as major characters? minor characters? in background and crowd scenes?) and roles (Who are the "good guys"? Who are the strong characters and the weak characters? Who is always being laughed at? Who is important?). Physical background, clothes, and general environment should also be examined critically. See Appendix A for sample worksheets.

This assignment could also be made using tapes of television shows made ten or twenty years ago if there is a museum or university in the vicinity which has such a collection. For an international media exercise, students might enjoy looking at *The BBC Summary of World Broadcasts*, which consists of translations of scripts of radio broadcasts made since 1939 and available on microfilm. This resource is described more fully in Chapter 6, in the section "Selected Primary Sources: Documents, Archives, and Research Collections."

Ethnographies

Ethnographies are descriptions of a culture and attempts to understand that culture from the point of view of its participants. They can be a useful and stimulating way to introduce students in a variety of courses to aspects of multiculturalism. Although the culture described can be that of a village in Samoa, it can also be that of the neighborhood barbershop, the teenagers' hangout on the corner, or the local senior citizen center. An ethnographic study on this level usually does not involve library research. The amount of time required can be controlled by adjusting the scope of the investigation.

Instructors not accustomed to assigning ethnographies may want to start by reading a small book by James P. Spradley and David W. McCurdy, *The Cultural Experience: Ethnography in a Complex Society*, which describes how the process of ethnographic research can be carried on by undergraduates. The book includes lists of potential subjects and several ethnographies written by undergraduate students.[11]

Among the subjects which have been successfully used for undergraduate ethnographies are weddings and religious observances; the manner in which parents treat girls and boys in public places such as department stores, grocery stores, and fast-food stores; observations of the student's peers in bars, in the library, or on line in the movies; grade school and high school classrooms and cafeterias; and nursery schools and airport arrival lounges.

In classes where learning about a multicultural world is an objective, ethnographic field work can be an extremely useful exercise. It not only enriches the researchers' understanding of the culture being studied, but it can also give the student researchers a new awareness of their own values by making them conscious of the implicit premises and tacit knowledge of our culture.

The ethnographic study can consist of observations, interviews, or both. As with all student research projects, care must be taken that the subject is small enough to be observable yet broad enough to offer some scope and to allow for meaningful observations or interviews.[12] If the subject of an ethnographic study has not been assigned, it is important that the instructor approve it before work begins. If interviews or participant observations are to be part of the study, students should learn the basic procedures for human-subject research. In addition, preapproval of questions by the instructor will help keep the study focused and should insure that questions are meaningful and not offensive. Alternatively, the class might work as a whole or in small groups to develop appropriate questions.

Interviews

Biographical studies based on interviews can be as useful in realizing multicultural objectives as such studies can be when library based. Results of the interviews can be written as a formal report, a journal entry, a newspaper article, a letter to the instructor, or a letter to a specific person who the student feels lacks understanding of what the interviewee represents. Regardless of the format in which the results of the interview are presented, the assignment can be limited to biographical information, or the student can be asked to place the life history of the interviewee into its historical context.

- In a foreign-language class, the student can interview immigrants or visitors from a country where that language is spoken. They can be asked about daily life, childhood, education, and popular culture in their home countries, and about their perceptions of the United States.

Such an interview is more likely to move the student in the direction of global understanding than is a chapter on "cultural background" in the average foreign-language textbook.

- In a mathematics or science class, students can interview members of the faculty in those departments or teachers of those subjects in local high schools. Subjects can be asked about their feelings for the subject, why they chose the field, what their experiences have been, what their research interests are, and their perceptions of career possibilities, specifically those for women and minorities, in their fields.

- A government class studying voting behavior can select specific groups (Jews, civil service workers, people over sixty, college students, etc.), interview individuals about their life histories, and then ask questions designed to elicit information on voting behavior and its reasons.

- Students studying twentieth-century history, sociology, health care, or the history of education or psychology can interview people who have been participants in or observers of relevant events or life styles.

Before doing the interviews, the class should discuss the kinds of questions that will be most likely to elicit the insights desired. The instructor will also want to insure that the possible relevance of issues such as gender, class, and ethnicity is discussed.

If time allows, results of the interviews can be presented as short oral reports. Sharing information with the class and being able to ask and answer questions are clear benefits of oral presentations. This is particularly true if a variety of groups and experiences are represented.

Photography and Videotape Projects

If the equipment is available, student projects employing still cameras or video cameras can be used effectively in a number of disciplines to further critical thinking, diversity, and even writing objectives. Working individually or in groups, students can provide photographs or brief videotapes to illustrate textbooks or classroom lectures in courses as different as urban sociology, child development, psychology of adolescence, primary education, history, health services administration, and marketing and retailing.

Prior to going out with a camera, the group should discuss the types of pictures which would be most effective in achieving their goals. Pictures can be prearranged and posed, or they can be candid, or a combination can be used. Students should be cautioned to remain flexible and to shoot many more pictures than will be ultimately required. Once the photographs have been developed, the group must decide which ones to include in the final project, write informative captions for them, and possibly write an explanation for the instructor discussing each photograph and how it illustrates or enriches the point made in the text or lecture.

The video camera provides the possibility of even more variety than does the still camera. In addition to making videotaped illustrations for textbooks or lectures, students can develop their own minidocumentaries. Filming can be done "on location" utilizing the "real world," or assembled sets and scripted dialogue can be used, or a combination of techniques can be employed. The writing of voice-over commentaries to explain and enrich the visual images will help students focus more sharply on the messages they want to convey. At the same time, it will reinforce the point that even this most modern and visual of formats requires the ability to write well.

Posters or Murals, and Leaflets or Brochures

Synthesizing information and translating it into a short, popular format is a useful exercise. Whether students actually write a leaflet or short brochure, or simply describe the contents and appearance of a projected mural or poster, such an exercise is a way to help students focus on the essence of an issue and how best to convey that essence to a specific audience. It can also provide instructive illustrations of the manner in which information generated in the academic world can be used in a broader context.

- A government class (or a composition class) can write leaflets and design posters and advertisements for certain political candidates, presenting the issues in such ways as to appeal most effectively to different audiences.
- An art class can decide what should be pictured on a mural in a specific housing project or library.
- A public-health class can design posters and brochures on the issues of AIDS, smoking, or childhood vaccination.
- An economics class can prepare a brochure with a suggested budget for a family on welfare.

- A literature class can write book jackets and advertising copy for the *New York Review of Books* and for the *Afro-American.*

- A music class can design posters to sell the latest recording of a Bach cantata or a rap group on the college campus.

Fictional Autobiographies

One way to help students picture the impact of events on "real" people is to have them construct a fictional autobiography. This is a project which in its simplest form might be based solely on class discussions and required readings, or it could include library research. As with so many of these alternative projects, the amount of work required can vary, and the information can be presented either orally or in writing.

One approach to this type of assignment is to have students adopt the identities of persons they wish could be represented in the class. In a course on nineteenth-century literature, the persons from that century could be a literary critic, a member of the intelligentsia, a member of the working class, a clergyman, a schoolteacher, a free Black, or a recent Irish immigrant. In an introductory economics class, the people represented could be a member of a trade union, an unemployed factory worker, a retired teacher, the owner of a small business, and the chief executive officer of a large corporation. The students can construct short autobiographies for their identities, choose names, and then be encouraged to make appropriate contributions to class discussions in that persona. If the people selected represent a variety of classes and ethnicities, students will themselves provide a constant "diversity mirror" through which to view the content of the course.

In a course which covers several historical periods, the assignment can become a family history. For a project described by Anderson and McClendon students in a course on the American family wrote five short papers focused on specific dates: 1720, 1800, 1870, 1935, and now. In the final paper the student assumes the role of a twenty-year-old living somewhere in the United States with a particular ethnic/racial identity, a gender, and an assigned family income. The first four papers trace the ancestors of that person. Questions addressed in each paper were the same and covered areas such as daily life, religious practices, training and treatment of children, and relationships among family members.[13] Similar projects could be used, with appropriate questions, in other courses which follow a chronological framework.

The Student as Teacher

Instructors well know that the best way to understand something is to have to teach it. Students can be given the same opportunity. The assignment can require either an individual student or members of a small group to present information to their classmates based on their own experiences or gained in their own multicultural research. This will probably work most effectively if the topics are narrow and the time allowed for the presentation is strictly limited. For this exercise to be effective, students must clearly understand the difference between giving an oral report and teaching the class.

Alternatively, students can be asked to present material which has already been covered in class as they would teach it to a group which is different from their own class. If the class is largely Hispanic and African American, how would they teach the lesson to a group of Jewish students? If the class is largely white and suburban, how would they present it to minority students in an inner-city high school? How would they teach it to a class in Bangladesh, France, or Saudi Arabia? Even if students decide they would cover the material in the same way in the new situation, thinking about the possibilities of doing it differently is a valuable exercise.

Electronic Mail

Finally, for campuses that are fully wired for the twenty-first century, e-mail offers students the diversity inherent in instant communication about any subject with their peers around the country and around the world. Where language differences do not form a barrier, they can become "pen pals" with other students from widely different regions and cultures. Thanks to today's electronic technology, students can experience the "global village" directly, without leaving home. See the section "Electronic Communication" in Chapter 6 for more information.

SHARING THE INFORMATION

When projects are assigned with a view to increasing the diversity content of the course, additional benefits will accrue if students can share with one another the results of their research. This can be done in several ways:

- If time in class cannot be spared, consider putting students' written projects (perhaps with your comments) on reserve in the library and requiring each member of the class to read at least two or three of them. Knowing that their peers will be reading their work and relying on them for information may give student authors an additional impetus for doing good work.

- If topics are in any way related to each other, part of a class session can be devoted to a panel discussion of the topics.

- If the development of writing skills is not a high priority, consider using one of the oral projects described previously in this chapter.

- If written reports are required, some students (or all, depending on class size and time available) can give five- or ten-minute oral summaries of their research to the class.

PLAGIARISM

The problem of students—from first year to postgraduate—handing in plagiarized papers continues to bedevil the academic world. Of course, there is never an absolute guarantee that any paper or project submitted will be original. However, the procedures described in the preceding chapter—the assignment of specific topics, instructor participation in the process via structured assignments and requirements for preliminary drafts, and the use of primary sources—as well as the use of the nontraditional formats which are described in this chapter, are fairly certain to forestall the use of term-paper mills or recycled student papers.

NOTES

1. These suggestions are adapted from Barbara Schneider Fuhrmann and Anthony F. Grasha, *A Practical Handbook for College Teachers* (Boston: Little, Brown, 1983), p. 160.

2. Ibid., p. 159.

3. Chet Meyers and Thomas B. Jones, *Promoting Active Learning: Strategies for the College Classroom* (San Francisco: Jossey-Bass, 1993), p. 94. The assignment is credited to Professor Loretta T. Johnson.

4. Dialogues as a writing assignment are described well in William Horrell, "Using Dialogues as Writing Assignments," *Innovation Abstracts* 14 (February 1992). Most of the specific dialogues mentioned come from Horrell's article.

5. David E. Stannard, *American Holocaust: Columbus and the Conquest of the New World* (New York: Oxford University Press, 1992), p. 210.

6. See Ivan Karp and Steven D. Lavine, "Museums Must Take on New Roles in This Multicultural Society," *Chronicle of Higher Education,* April 14, 1993, p. B3; and Ivan Karp and Steven D. Lavine, eds., *The Poetics and Politics of Museum Display* (Washington, DC: Smithsonian Institution Press, 1991).

7. The example is from Racism and Sexism Resource Center for Educators, *Stereotypes, Distortions, and Omissions in U.S. History Textbooks* (New York: Council on Interracial Books for Children, 1977), p. 125.

8. The phrase "guided fantasies" and this exercise are from Nancy J. Davis, "Teaching about Inequality: Student Resistance, Paralysis, and Rage," *Teaching Sociology* 20 (July 1992): 235.

9. This exercise was described by Margie L. Kidder Edwards in a personal letter dated January 18, 1994.

10. In relation to this assignment, instructors might want to look at Stetson Kennedy, *Jim Crow Guide: The Way It Was* (Boca Raton: Florida Atlantic University Press, 1959, 1990), a somewhat tongue-in-cheek tour through the South before the desegregation laws.

11. See James P. Spradley and David W. McCurdy, *The Cultural Experience: Ethnography in a Complex Society* (Chicago: Science Research Associates, 1972). Written for undergraduates, this book offers a clear explanation of how to do urban ethnographies and contains examples of student work. Instructors interested in exploring student ethnographies further will find Spradley's later books, *The Ethnographic Interview* (New York: Holt, Rinehart, and Winston, 1979) and *Participant Observation* (New York: Holt, Rinehart, and Winston, 1980), interesting.

12. Some of these subjects were suggested by Phyllis Bronstein and Michele Paludi, "The Introductory Psychology Course from a Broader Human Perspective," in Phyllis Bronstein and Katheryn Quina, eds., *Teaching a Psychology of People: Resources for Gender and Sociocultural Awareness* (Washington, DC: American Psychological Association, 1988).

13. Katheryn Anderson and John McClendon, "Historical Perspectives: The American Family," in Myra Dinnerstein and Betty Schmitz, eds., *Ideas and Resources for Integrating Women's Studies into the Curriculum* (Tucson: University of Arizona Press, 1986).

5

Student Reactions
and Interactions

This chapter discusses the possibility of student resistance to multiculturalism in the classroom and offers some practical suggestions for dealing with this reaction.

EXPECT SOME PROBLEMS

It is wise to be prepared for occasional hostility from some students when issues of ethnicity, class, and gender are included in your course. Whether or not you will actually experience the problems discussed in this section may depend on the numbers and types of diversity-related projects selected, as well as on variables ranging from the area of the country in which the institution is located, to your own background, to the manner in which the course is described in the catalog, and probably—to an extent that we prefer not to contemplate—chance. This discussion is provided so that instructors can be aware of some of the possible reactions students may have to the issue of diversity. Preparing for these potential problems in advance should help instructors feel more comfortable about attempting to use some of the ideas presented in this book.[1]

The problems encountered in courses clearly labeled as being concerned with women, minorities, or other issues of diversity will be different from those encountered in courses without such labels. In traditional courses the problems arise when issues and foci usually seen as peripheral are moved to the core and when students perceive such issues as irrelevant to the "real" content. The challenge to the instructor is to help students understand that this broader inclusiveness is essential if one is to achieve accuracy in understanding the subject of the course.

Problems related to course content that are frequently reported in the literature are reflected in comments such as:

- "I signed up for a course in marriage and the family; why are we talking about Blacks?"

- "Are we going to talk about women today, or are we going to learn something?"

- "I'm sick of hearing about the poor and the elderly. Can't we just talk about ordinary people?"

- "It's not true that Blacks and Hispanics are discriminated against in hiring; where I work they always get the best jobs even if they don't know anything."

- "When will we stop talking about "those people" and talk about the important things?"

In addition to raising questions about the content of the course, discussions of race, gender, and other aspects of diversity can be expected to elicit strong emotional feelings from many students. Lisa Whitten has provided a useful list of emotional reactions to racial and cultural materials which one often encounters from students:

- Ethnocentricity and lack of empathy: This is a particularly common reaction among white males who feel most threatened, feel they really know it all, or feel they are being picked on. Children and grandchildren of immigrants from Europe will say, "We made it—why can't they?" The idea that being an African American, a Native American, or a Hispanic American is different from being a white immigrant is seen as ridiculous. Lack of empathy can also be seen when individual groups appear to vie for the title of most victimized, as in comments directed to Jews: "You're white! What do you know about discrimination?"

- Denial of the problem: Students will say, "We are all just Americans now; these are problems of the past."

- Defensiveness: Students will claim, "I didn't do anything to you. Why blame me?" or "Just because you are a Black doesn't mean you are more sensitive to racial issues than I am."

- Frustration and anger: African American students will say, "Don't make me speak for all of my race." Other students may complain,

"You said you wanted to teach a course which was truly inclusive, yet you haven't mentioned the problems of gays and lesbians once." Others may complain, "I thought I was going to learn about the history of the South; instead, I am learning to feel guilty because my ancestors owned slaves."

- Acting out: Students may blame the teacher or call other students names.[2]

SOME SUGGESTED APPROACHES TO CLASSROOM PROBLEMS RELATED TO ISSUES OF DIVERSITY

Below are some approaches which have been reported to be useful in these sensitive situations. The list is only meant to be suggestive. Instructors need to experiment with a variety of strategies and adopt those with which they are comfortable.

- State at the outset that some issues, not usually discussed in our society, will arise during your mutual search for a broader, more accurate, more inclusive picture. Acknowledge the discomfort—or lack of practice in this type of discourse—and establish clear guidelines for classroom discussion.
- Forestall some discomfort in dealing with controversial topics by having the presentation made by students. This removes the instructor from the role of authority and allows students more freedom.
- Provide activities and discussion topics which will enable students to begin to develop a measure of empathy for other groups.
- Deal directly with the problem of students' perceiving certain topics as being peripheral by reiterating and reinforcing the importance of the topics in your thinking and emphasizing their relationship to the overall subject of the course. Ultimately, the instructor is the authority who defines the subject, and if it is clearly important to you, it is more likely to be accepted as important by the students. Inclusion of diversity-related questions in tests is a further statement of its importance.
- Place the increased attention to minorities and women within the context of the history both of the discipline and of higher education.
- Provide opportunities for students to discuss variations from the norm. Students' own experiences which vary from theoretical or statistical pictures need to be acknowledged and discussed.

- Not unexpectedly, discussions of sensitive issues can build up pressure in the classroom. Students become emotionally involved and are also worried about grades. Teachers are concerned about control and about evaluations by students and peers. It is sometimes best if the instructor can openly acknowledge the tension. In fact, the instructor might even refer to the level of tension as an indication of the importance of the sensitive issues being discussed. If these issues can evoke such reactions in a college classroom, perhaps students can begin to understand why and how they can lead to explosive behavior by various groups in our society.

- It is possible to help with feelings of guilt (about whiteness, economic security, etc.) by discussing the difference between a recognition of the facts and an acceptance of personal responsibility for the events which occurred.

- Try an anonymous midsemester evaluation of the course by students using a prepared form. Such an evaluation is described by Becky Thompson and Estelle Disch. They recommend using a form that asks the students to describe what they like and don't like about the course, how the teacher or classmates could make the course better, and what factors make them comfortable or uncomfortable when participating in class discussion. The innovative aspect of the authors' procedure is the recommendation that after the anonymously completed forms are collected, they are redistributed randomly to the class. Students' reactions and comments are then shared by having each one read another student's responses aloud.[3]

Finally, establish clear guidelines for classroom discussions. It is important to acknowledge that acceptable behavior is defined differently in different cultures, places, groups, and even by different instructors within the same institution. Most students recognize that acceptable classroom behavior is different from that at home or in the cafeteria, but it is important to specify what is acceptable in this particular class. This is especially important if controversial or difficult topics will be discussed. Some instructors find it useful to have the students draw up rules for acceptable behavior within the context of the specific class. Among the issues which might be addressed in this context are

- Confidentiality: Students need to be assured that personal comments will not be repeated outside of the classroom.

- Teacher openness: Instructors should be ready to talk about their own struggles, to apologize when it's appropriate, or to change directions when the desired outcomes are not achieved. Midsemester anonymous evaluations are useful in this regard.

- Clear acknowledgment of the basis for grading: Instructors need to make their standards clear. They should emphasize that although a willingness to discuss issues is important, agreement with classmates or the instructor is *not* needed to get a good grade.

- Participation: Although class participation is encouraged, people have a right to remain silent, as long as that silence is not the result of being unprepared.

- Opinions: Everyone is entitled to an opinion, but there is a difference between an opinion unsupported by any facts and an informed opinion. There is no value to an opinion based on uninformed prejudices.

- Respect: Insulting language or personal attacks will not be permitted. Students need to believe that their comments will be treated with respect by their peers and by the instructor. They also need to be sure that the instructor will remain in control and protect them from personal attacks.[4]

NOTES

1. Among the many discussions of these issues are Donna Crawley and Martha Ecker, "Integrating Issues of Gender, Race, and Ethnicity into Experimental Psychology and Other Social-Science Methodology Courses," *Women's Studies Quarterly* 18, nos. 1, 2 (1990): 105–116; Martha Goodman, "Teaching New Ways to Think about Race, Class, and Gender," in Patricia Hill Collins and Margaret L. Andersen, eds., *An Inclusive Curriculum: Race, Class, and Gender in Sociological Instruction* (Washington, DC: American Sociological Association, 1987), pp. 7–12; Lisa Whitten, "Managing Student Reactions to Controversial Issues in the College Classroom," *Transformations* 4 (spring 1993): 30–44; Lynn Weber Cannon, "Fostering Positive Race, Class, and Gender Dynamics in the Classroom," *Women's Studies Quarterly* 18 (1990): 126–134; and Paula Rothenberg, "Teaching 'Racism and Sexism in a Changing America,' " *Radical Teacher* 27 (1984): 2–5. (The writer has noted—through our prism of diversity—that all the foregoing writers are women.)

2. Whitten, "Managing Student Reactions," pp. 33–36.

3. Becky Thompson and Estelle Disch, "Feminist, Anti-racist, Anti-oppression Teaching: Two White Women's Experience," *Radical Teacher* 41 (spring 1992): 7.

4. These suggestions are adapted from Cannon, "Fostering Positive Race, Class, and Gender Dynamics."

II
Resources

6

Resources for Students and Instructors

This chapter contains a selection of resources which will be helpful to faculty when devising the teaching strategies and types of student projects discussed in Part I of this book, and to students undertaking those projects. The lists of resources are meant to be suggestive only: They are far from complete and are not necessarily a selection which would be best for every purpose. Although few libraries will have all of these books, most midsize college libraries should have a reasonable number of them.

For instructors who need to go beyond the basic sources discussed in this chapter, the next chapter contains advice about effective and efficient use of the online catalog when doing research on multicultural topics. The annotated bibliography includes additional general titles, as well as scholarly monographs and articles, many of which discuss diversifying the curriculum in specific disciplines.

The lists in this chapter are arranged by types of information rather than by subject. It is hoped that this arrangement will be useful for those who are browsing for ideas and might make decisions about student projects based on the types of resources available, as well as for those seeking sources of specific information. This chapter is arranged in eleven sections:

1. "Encyclopedias and Other Overviews" annotates sources which can provide a fast overview of aspects of the history and culture of specific groups in the United States and elsewhere. The number of works of this type has grown greatly in recent years, and this list contains only a representative sample.

2. "Directories" is valuable in selecting organizations and associations, and newspapers and journals, either as subjects for research projects or as sources of information.

3. "Chronologies and Atlases" is recommended if there is a need to establish basic facts about time and place.

4. "Statistics" lists compendiums of statistics about the United States and other countries. Instructors looking for a fast way to incorporate some basic information about other countries, as well as specific ethnic groups in our country, will find this section useful.

5. "Biographies and Biographical Directories" provides sources which will enable students or instructors to locate suitable subjects for student research into the lives of people representative of specific groups, interests, occupations, or regions. It also lists some sources of basic biographical information about women and members of minority groups.

6. "Periodicals: Ethnic Press of the United States, Foreign Press, and Specialized Periodical Indexes" includes sources of information to locate full-text newspapers and discusses some indexes which can be used with a variety of periodicals.

7. "Selected Primary Sources: Newspapers and Magazines of the Nineteenth and Early Twentieth Centuries" serves the needs of instructors who would like to use this category of primary sources.

8. "Selected Primary Sources: Documents, Archives, and Research Collections" discusses sources ranging from single-volume collections of letters or documents to archives in multireel microfilm sets.

9. "Visual Sources: Films, Videos, Photographs, and Posters" is helpful in structuring assignments using cartoons, documentary photographs, posters, or portraits, and in locating sources of films and videos.

10. "Sample Syllabi" lists books, documents, and articles which contain syllabi devised by instructors in various disciplines. Methods of locating additional syllabi are also described.

11. "Electronic Communication" briefly comments on listservs, e-mail, and the Internet.

1. ENCYCLOPEDIAS AND OTHER OVERVIEWS

Dictionary of Afro-American Slavery. Edited by Randall M. Miller and John David Smith. New York: Greenwood, 1988.
A substantial and scholarly volume covering the period from the first English settlements to Reconstruction. Some articles are quite lengthy; all have bibliographies.

Dictionary of American Immigration History. Edited by Francesco Cordasco. Metuchen, NJ: Scarecrow, 1990.

Dictionary of Asian American History. Edited by Hyung-Chan Kim. New York: Greenwood, 1986.

Dictionary of Mexican American History. Edited by Matt S. Meier and Feliciano Rivera. Westport, CT: Greenwood, 1981.

Dictionary of Native American Literature. Edited by Andrew Wiget. New York: Garland, 1994.
Comprehensive and authoritative articles treating the oral and written components of Native American literature. Articles on individual authors are included along with topical essays. Extensive bibliographies.

Encyclopedia of African-American Civil Rights: From Emancipation to the Present. Edited by Charles D. Lowery and John F. Marszalek. New York: Greenwood, 1992.
With over eight hundred short articles on individuals, organizations, events, and court cases from 1861 on, this volume will be helpful to students and instructors looking for research topics. The brief entries give just enough information to arouse interest. Chronology and bibliographies.

Encyclopedia of American Social History. Edited by Mary Kupiec Cayton, Elliott J. Gorn, and Peter W. Williams. 3 vols. New York: Charles Scribner's Sons, 1993.
Organized into broad thematic sections which include periods of social change; the construction of social identity; ethnic and racial subcultures; work and labor; and social problems, social control, and social protest, this set is composed of substantial, well-written, scholarly articles. Highly recommended.

Encyclopedia of World Cultures. Edited by David Levinson. 10 vols. Boston: G. K. Hall, 1991.
Signed scholarly articles discuss 1,500 cultural groups in this ambitious publication. Each article addresses issues of history and cultural

relations, settlements, economy, kinship, marriage and family, sociopolitical organization, and religion. Much of the material is derived from the Human Relations Area Files.

Harvard Encyclopedia of American Ethnic Groups. Edited by Stephen Thernstrom et al. Cambridge, MA: Harvard University Press, 1980. This is the most comprehensive one-volume reference book on the subject and, despite its age, is still the most frequently cited. More than one hundred contributors describe 106 ethnic groups and also provide many useful overview articles. Among the most relevant of these general articles are those on American identity, concepts of ethnicity, assimilation and pluralism, education, family patterns, immigration, intermarriage, language maintenance, leadership, politics, and religion. Highly recommended for one-stop information.

Hirschfelder, Arlene, and Martha Kreipe de Montano. *The Native American Almanac: A Portrait of Native America Today.* New York: Prentice Hall, 1993.
A small, popularly written compendium which includes a chronology and a useful list of Native American autobiographies from the mid-nineteenth century on.

Hispanic American Almanac: A Reference Work on Hispanics in the United States. Edited by Nicolas Kanellos. Detroit: Gale, 1993.
A popular, encyclopedia-like resource containing essays, illustrations, biographies, and bibliographies. Includes historic overviews, significant documents, lists of historic landmarks, and articles on language, theater, art, films, and so on. The descriptions of popular Hispanic American newspapers and periodicals and good lists of Hispanic Americans prominent in various fields are particularly useful.

Johnson, John W. *Historic U.S. Court Cases, 1690–1990: An Encyclopedia.* New York: Garland, 1992.
Summarizes and discusses the cases, placing each in its historic context, with bibliographies included for each case. The style is sometimes a bit dull, but an attempt was made not to use legalese. Part IV, "Race and Gender in American Law" discusses thirty-one important cases, and an additional forty are in Part V, "Civil Liberties." This volume is a good place to start when looking for relevant cases.

Native America in the Twentieth Century: An Encyclopedia. Edited by Mary B. Davis. New York: Garland, 1994.

Almost three hundred specialists from many areas have contributed to this exceptionally balanced and authoritative overview of Native Americans in this century. The brief bibliographies and many cross references add to the value of this volume. Highly recommended.

The Negro Almanac: A Reference Work on the African-American. Edited by Harry A. Ploski and James Williams. 5th ed. Detroit: Gale, 1989. A basic, popularly written, single-volume source of information.

2. DIRECTORIES

Gale Information Directories. Detroit: Gale.
Asian Americans Information Directory. 1994–95.
Hispanic Americans Information Directory. 1990–91.
Native Americans Information Directory. 1993.
Each directory in this series is comprehensive and should prove helpful in many situations. Included are lists of library collections, videos, publishers, newspapers, and newsletters, associations, services, agencies, and research centers. Most lists are annotated. The lists of video titles and newspapers should prove particularly useful. Highly recommended.

Gonzales, Sylvia Alicia. *Hispanic American Voluntary Organizations.* Westport, CT: Greenwood, 1985.
Nearly two hundred organizations are described in entries which range up to ten pages. Each entry includes the history of the organization and the names of founders and important members. Also included are a subject index and chronologies of Mexican Americans, Puerto Ricans, and Cuban Americans. Although perhaps dated as a directory, this volume is still useful as history and as a source of names and dates.

Guide to Multicultural Resources. Edited by Charles A. Taylor. Madison, WI: Praxis Publishers, 1993.
The resources are names of organizations that are arranged by ethnic group, with a geographical index permitting researchers to locate nearby groups. The listings are well annotated and include organizations related to art, education, libraries, media, religion, women, and so on. Names of newspapers and periodicals are included in the media sections. This volume could be helpful to students looking for organizations or groups to study.

Minority Organizations: A National Directory. 4th ed. Garrett Park, MD: Garrett Park Press, 1992.

Alphabetically arranged by name of organization, the entries are annotated. Although the geographic index is helpful, the index by subject and service area is not as complete as it could be.

3. CHRONOLOGIES AND ATLASES

Allen, James Paul, and Eugene J. Turner, eds. *We the People: An Atlas of America's Ethnic Diversity*. New York: Macmillan, 1988.
Maps, charts, and an extensive text which includes information on history, immigration patterns, housing, employment, and language. Based on 1980 census.

Grun, Bernard. *The Timetables of History: A Horizontal Linkage of People and Events*. 3rd ed. New York: Simon & Schuster, 1991.
Although clearly reflecting the German origin of its original, this volume allows one to see "what else was happening" at the time. Columns include history and politics, culture, science and technology, and everyday life.

Hornsby, Alton, Jr. *Chronology of African-American History: Significant Events and People from 1619 to the Present*. Detroit: Gale, 1991.
Although arranged by year, month, and date, this chronology is in narrative form. The index is mostly names, although some subjects are included (e.g., riots, the Ku Klux Klan, and interracial marriage). This volume might be useful for locating potential research projects.

Mattson, Mark T. *Atlas of the 1990 Census*. New York: Macmillan, 1992.
Part IV, "Race and Ethnicity," provides information on race and ethnic population down to county level. Well-drawn, colorful, informative maps and charts, but no narrative text.

Peters, Arno. *Peters Atlas of the World*. New York: Harper & Row, 1990.
An extremely valuable atlas. Highlights include the world in forty-three maps drawn to the same scale, world maps with the equator in the middle of the page, and thematic maps which include religion, health, language, and economics. Not widely available, but worth an effort to locate.

Sloan, Irving J. *The Jews in America, 1621–1977: A Chronology and Fact Book*. Dobbs Ferry, NY: Oceana, 1978.

Tung, William L. *The Chinese in America, 1820–1973: A Chronology and Fact Book*. Dobbs Ferry, NY: Oceana, 1974.

Waldman, Carl. *Atlas of the North American Indian*. Maps and illustrations by Molly Braun. New York: Facts on File, 1985.

A short, popularly written dictionary most useful for its appendices, which include a chronology of North-American Indian history, a list of Indian tribes with historical and contemporary locations, and a list of federal and state reservations.

4. STATISTICS

Historical Statistics of the United States, Colonial Times to 1970. White Plains, NY: Kraus International, 1989.
   Although statistics from the early periods are scanty, this is an extremely useful compendium.

Mitchell, B. R. *European Historical Statistics, 1750–1975.* 2nd ed. New York: Facts on File, 1980.

————. *International Historical Statistics: Africa and Asia.* New York: New York University Press, 1982.

Negro Population, 1790–1915. Washington, DC: Government Printing Office, 1918. Reprinted as *Negro Population in the United States, 1790–1915.* New York: Arno Press, 1968.
   Originally published by the Bureau of the Census, the narratives and statistics collected in this extensive collection reflect the attitudes of an earlier period, as well as providing a wealth of fascinating statistical detail.

Statistical Abstract of Latin America. Edited by James W. Wilkie. Los Angeles: UCLA Latin American Center Publications. Annual.
   Covers the countries of South America and Central America, plus Cuba, Haiti, and the Dominican Republic. A statistical compendium drawn from various sources, this annual publication makes good use of graphs and cartograms, as well as charts. There is a detailed subject index.

Statistical Abstract of the United States. Washington, DC: Government Printing Office. Annual.
   The basic statistical publication about the United States, this annual volume includes thousands of social, economic, and demographic statistics.

Statistical Handbook on U.S. Hispanics. Edited by Frank L. Schick and Renee Schick. Phoenix, AZ: Oryx, 1991.

Statistical Handbook on Women in America. Edited by Cynthia Taeuber. Phoenix, AZ: Oryx, 1991.
   Both volumes contain a multitude of statistics drawn from federal government sources. Latest data are from 1988.

Statistical Record of Asian Americans. Detroit: Gale, 1993.
Statistical Record of Black America. Detroit: Gale, 1990.
Statistical Record of Hispanic Americans. Detroit: Gale, 1993.
Statistical Record of Native North Americans. Detroit: Gale, 1993.
> This series is somewhat more extensive than the one listed above since it draws on figures from a wide range of private as well as government organizations. The volume on Black America, for example, has charts ranging from the attitudes of eighth graders toward school, to data on winning baseball pitchers, to standard vital statistics.

Statistical Record of Women Worldwide. Detroit: Gale, 1991.
> Statistics on most conceivable topics (Girl Scouts, women clergy, life expectancy, etc.). Tables are taken from many sources, so that coverage by country is uneven. A good index facilitates locating statistics about particular countries.

Statistical Yearbook/Annuaire statistique. New York: United Nations Department of Economic and Social Development. Annual.
> Although there tends to be a two- to five-year time lag in the publishing of these statistics, this United Nations publication remains the best single-volume source for worldwide social, demographic, and economic statistics. Includes some unexpected charts: for example, newsprint consumption in kilograms per 1,000 inhabitants (ranges from a low of 7 in Mozambique to a high of 58,000 in New Zealand).

Stuart, Paul. *Nations Within a Nation: Historical Statistics of American Indians.* New York: Greenwood, 1987.
> A variety of statistics drawn from many sources include actual counts and estimates of demography, education, property, and health. Some charts go back to the early nineteenth century; most start with the late nineteenth century.

5. BIOGRAPHIES AND BIOGRAPHICAL DIRECTORIES

Addis, Patricia K. *Through a Woman's I: An Annotated Bibliography of American Women's Autobiographical Writings, 1946–1976.* Metuchen, NJ: Scarecrow, 1983.
> An index to autobiographical books and collections of letters. There is a subject index and an index to the authors by profession or other salient characteristic.

Arksey, Laura, Nancy Pries, and Marcia Reed. *American Diaries: An Annotated Bibliography of Published American Diaries and Journals.* Vol. 1, *Diaries Written from 1492–1844.* Vol. 2, *Diaries Written from 1845–1980.* Detroit: Gale, 1983–1987.

This well-annotated and exhaustive set is particularly useful because it includes less than book-length items. The detailed subject index includes entries such as plantation management, Jews, slaves, Indians, and immigrants (by country). The name index includes people mentioned in the diaries as well as the authors of the diaries.

Bataille, Gretchen M., and Kathleen Mullen Sands. *American Indian Women: Telling Their Lives.* Lincoln: University of Nebraska Press, 1984.

A discussion of the biographies, not a compilation or directory. Good annotated bibliography includes a list of autobiographies, a list of biographies, and a list of ethnographic studies.

Brignano, Russel C. *Black Americans in Autobiography: An Annotated Bibliography of Autobiographies and Autobiographical Books Written since the Civil War.* Rev. and exp. ed. Durham, NC: Duke University Press, 1984.

The subtitle of this book is misleading since 42 of the 668 books annotated were published before the Civil War. The inclusion of a checklist of autobiographies written before 1865 and reprinted after 1945 makes it easier to locate reprint editions of these works. Indexed topics include activities, experiences, occupations, professions, organizations, locations, and institutions.

Brumble, H. David. *An Annotated Bibliography of American Indian and Eskimo Autobiographies.* Lincoln: University of Nebraska Press, 1981.

Contemporary Black Biography: Profiles from the International Black Community. Detroit: Gale. Annual.

Serving as a supplement to the publisher's well-established series *Contemporary Biography*, annual volumes in this new series provide short, fast, popular, illustrated biographies of famous or well-known Black people, as well as "those not yet household names" who are also deemed to be important and influential. The first volume (1992) includes a small number of individuals from earlier in the century whose influence continues to be felt today. Good source for people in show business, sports, music, and politics. Valuable cumulative indexes to nationality, occupation, subjects, and names are provided.

Dictionary of American Negro Biography. Edited by Rayford W. Logan and Michael R. Winston. New York: Norton, 1982.

First Person Female American: A Selected and Annotated Bibliography of the Autobiographies of American Women Living after 1950. Edited by Carolyn H. Rhodes. Troy, NY: Whitston Publishing, 1980.

Greene, Victor R. *American Immigrant Leaders, 1800–1910: Marginality and Identity.* Baltimore, MD: Johns Hopkins University Press, 1987. A short, readable discussion of leaders of major nineteenth-century immigrant groups, this volume could be a starting point for biographical studies of immigrant leaders.

Holt, Hamilton, ed. *The Life Stories of Undistinguished Americans as Told by Themselves.* With a new introduction by Werner Sollors. New York: Routledge, 1990. Original stories taken from among seventy-five autobiographies published in *The Independent* from 1902 to 1906. The first edition of this book was published in 1906. Included are the life stories of a Polish girl working in a sweatshop, a Greek peddler, an Irish cook, a German girl working as a nurse, a Japanese servant, a Chinese man, a southern white woman, a southern "Colored" woman, and others. This edition includes a list of reviews of the original edition.

Kanellos, Nichols. *Biographical Dictionary of Hispanic Literature in the United States: The Literature of Puerto Ricans, Cuban Americans, and Other Hispanic Writers.* Westport, CT: Greenwood, 1989.

Kaplan, Louis. *A Bibliography of American Autobiographies.* Madison: University of Wisconsin Press, 1961. An annotated bibliography of autobiographies separately published before 1945. The subject index includes occupations, places, and important historical events. There are many entries for immigrants, listed by place of origin. Although old, this work is particularly useful because all 781 books discussed are available on microfiche in *American Autobiographies: Autobiographies Cited in Louis Kaplan's "Bibliography of American Autobiographies"* (La Crosse, WI: Brookhaven Press, 1974).

Littlefield, Daniel F., Jr., and James W. Parins. *A Biobibliography of Native American Writers, 1772–1924.* Metuchen, NJ: Scarecrow, 1981; supplement, 1985.

Notable Black American Women. Detroit: Gale, 1992.

Notable Hispanic American Women. Detroit: Gale, 1993.

Each of these volumes has several hundred entries varying in length from 500 to 2,500 words; most have bibliographies. Indexes by occupation and by ethnicity are included.

O'Connell, Agnes N., and Nancy Felipe Russo, eds. *Models of Achievement: Reflections of Eminent Women in Psychology*. New York: Columbia University Press, 1983.

Informal, well-written autobiographical accounts by seventeen prominent women psychologists. There is an excellent historical introduction (with bibliography) and a concluding chapter which discusses patterns of achievement, isolating such factors as family background, parents' occupations, and marital and motherhood status. An excellent model for this type of publication, this work could serve as an example for student group projects involving individual biographies.

Siegel, Patricia Joan, and Kay Thomas Finley. *Women in the Scientific Search: An American Biobibliography, 1724–1979*. Metuchen, NJ: Scarecrow, 1985.

Brief biographical sketches and bibliographic information for 250 women.

Slave Narratives

Slave narratives constitute a particular class of biographical work; they can be true fiction, fictionalized truth, "as told to" stories, true autobiography, or oral history. Frequently possessing an immediacy and a poignancy which are lacking in secondary sources, these narratives can serve as the basis of many different student projects.

Davis, Charles T., and Henry Louis Gates, Jr., eds. *The Slave's Narrative*. Oxford: Oxford University Press, 1985.

A collection of articles assessing slave narratives as history and as literature, this is a valuable introduction to these sources. The article "The Art and Science of Reading WPA Slave Narratives" by Paul D. Escott, which is included, would be helpful to undergraduates using the Rawick collection below.

Rawick, George P., ed. *The American Slave: A Composite Autobiography*. 19 vols. Westport, CT: Greenwood, 1972. Supplement: Series 1, 12 vols., 1977; Series 2, 10 vols., 1977.

This collection contains the oral recollections of former slaves first

collected by researchers from Fisk University and Hampton Institute
in the late 1920s and later by WPA researchers.

Locating additional slave narratives. The work by Brignano, cited above,
contains some slave narratives. Additional ones can be located in
libraries by doing a key word search for SLAVES and BIOGRA-
PHY. For more information on effective use of the online catalog
see Chapter 7.

6. PERIODICALS: ETHNIC PRESS OF THE UNITED STATES, FOREIGN PRESS, AND SPECIALIZED PERIODICAL INDEXES

Directories

In addition to the directories listed here, the Gale Information Directories, described above in the section "Directories" is a good source for
locating current ethnic publications in the United States.

The African Book World and Press: A Directory. Compiled by the African
Book Publishing Record. Edited by Hans M. Zell. 4th ed. Oxford:
Hans Zell Publishers, 1989.
This directory is the standard guide to publishing in Africa. Includes
a subject index to periodicals and magazines, a list of the principal
dealers in African books in Europe and the United States, and lists
of libraries, publishers, and major periodicals and newspapers.

*International Literary Market Place: The Directory of the International
Book Publishing Industry.* New Providence, NJ: Bowker. Annual.
A directory of large and small publishers from 180 countries. Since
the index by type of publisher has a section for college textbooks,
this annual publication is one way of locating textbooks from other
countries. There is also a subject index which enables one, for
example, to locate publishers of books about anthropology in Ghana,
about behavioral sciences in Saudi Arabia, or about business in India.
Listings include the number of titles published each year and tele-
phone, telex, and fax numbers.

Ireland, Sandra L. Jones. *Ethnic Periodicals in Contemporary America:
An Annotated Guide.* New York: Greenwood, 1990.
Although meant primarily for writers looking for publishing oppor-
tunities, the information supplied is valuable to researchers. Brief

descriptions, circulation size, and prices are included for almost three hundred periodicals from one hundred ethnic groups.

Katz, William A., and Linda Sternberg Katz. *Magazines for Libraries: For the General Reader and School, Junior College, College, University, and Public Libraries.* 7th ed. New York: Bowker, 1992.
A basic list of periodicals in all subject areas.

Willings Press Guide: A Guide to the Press of the United Kingdom and to the Principal Publications of Europe, the Americas, Australasia, Asia, Africa and the Middle East. Vol. 1: *The United Kingdom.* Vol. 2: *Overseas.* West Sussex, England: Reed Information Services. Annual.
The *Overseas* volume lists publishers by country and classifies them under more than 250 headings. Although some academic and scholarly journals are included, this guide is largely a listing of general-interest and occupationally oriented newspapers and magazines. This directory will be useful for instructors seeking English-language newspapers from other countries. Ordering directions and costs are included for all entries.

Locating the Periodicals

If your library does not own the periodical needed, talk to the interlibrary loan department. Periodicals owned by thousands of libraries can now be located, and copies of articles requested, through online bibliographic databases and through commercial document delivery services. Microfilm, too, is often available on interlibrary loan.

The most comprehensive source for ascertaining whether or not a periodical is available in microform is:

Guide to Microforms in Print. Westport, CT: Microform Review. Annual.

The following two compilations of newspapers are particularly suitable for undergraduate research.

Editorials on File. New York: Facts on File.
A twice-a-month publication, this service provides full-scale reproductions of editorials from 150 newspapers in the United States and Canada. Topics selected for coverage are those most in the news. Although not concerned specifically with issues of multiculturalism, this publication will yield much interesting material. Very simple to use.

Ethnic Newswatch. CD-ROM database. Stamford, CT: Softline Information.

A unique and valuable resource, this CD-ROM database is composed of full-text articles from a wide variety of ethnic newspapers, including Asian American, Jewish, Native American, Hispanic, Middle-Eastern American, and European American. The database goes back to 1991 and adds about 2,500 new articles a month. Book, movie, theater, and record reviews are included.

Specialized Periodical Indexes

In addition to using the more general online, CD-ROM, and print indexes, such as *Social Science Index, Public Affairs Information Service (PAIS),* and *America: History and Life,* students and instructors will find the following more specialized indexes useful.

Alternative Press Index: An Index to Alternative and Radical Publications. College Park, MD: Alternative Press Centre, 1969–. Quarterly.

This index is devoted to limited-circulation periodicals covering subjects such as Marxist theory, gay and lesbian rights, environmental concerns, atheism, animal rights, alternative cultures, citizen activism, seniors, labor, and the Third World.

Chicano Database. CD-ROM database. Berkeley: University of California at Berkeley, Chicano Studies Library, 1990–. Semiannual.

Includes citations to books, articles in collections, reports, and journal articles. Subject interests include art, literature, sociology, psychology, and public affairs. Forty periodicals are indexed fully, and about three hundred are indexed selectively. Some materials are included here which are not included in the *Chicano Index,* discussed below, and this version is much easier to use.

The Chicano Index: A Comprehensive Subject, Author, and Title Index to Chicano Materials. Berkeley: University of California at Berkeley, Chicano Studies Library, 1981–. Quarterly. Earlier title: *Chicano Periodical Index.*

This print version of the Chicano Database is not as inclusive as the database.

Hispanic American Periodical Index (HAPI). Los Angeles: UCLA Latin American Center Publications, 1975–. Annual.

Indexes 350 social science and humanities journals.

Index to Black Periodicals. Boston: G. K. Hall, 1950–. Annual. Early issues were called *Index to Periodical Articles by and about Blacks* and *Index to Periodical Articles by and about Negroes*.

This specialized service indexes thirty to thirty-five general and academic periodicals whose primary focus is Africa and African American concerns. It does not include articles by or about those subjects which appear in more general journals.

Women Studies Abstracts. Rush, NY: Rush Publishing, 1972–. Quarterly. Variant title: *Women's Studies Abstracts*.

The number of journals and the number of issues of each journal that are indexed in each issue of this service vary, although usually about thirty titles are covered. Journals indexed are those whose primary emphasis is women studies; look elsewhere for articles about women which appear in other sources.

7. SELECTED PRIMARY SOURCES: NEWSPAPERS AND MAGAZINES OF THE NINETEENTH AND EARLY TWENTIETH CENTURIES

Directories and Discussions

American Periodicals, 1741–1900: An Index to the Microfilm Collections. Edited by Jean Hoornstra and Trudy Heath. Ann Arbor, MI: University Microfilms International, 1979.

One of the best guides to eighteenth- and nineteenth-century American periodicals, this volume includes descriptions of content, intended audience, names of editors, and size of circulation for over 1,100 periodicals. Informative, detailed subject index. The microform collection itself is described below in this section.

Bullock, Penelope L. *The Afro-American Periodical Press, 1838–1909*. Baton Rouge: Louisiana State University Press, 1981.

This guide contains full descriptions of the content and publishing history of the journals listed.

Daniel, Walter C. *Black Journals of the United States*. Westport, CT: Greenwood, 1982.

Historical and descriptive profiles of more than one hundred African American journals published from 1827 to the 1980s. An interesting "Chronology of Significant Events in African American History" with listings of journals started during each period is included. This volume would be an efficient starting point for students because of the extensive annotations and bibliographies for each title. Information about indexing and estimates of circulation are included in the annotations.

Danky, James P., ed. *Native American Periodicals and Newspapers, 1828–1982: Bibliography, Publishing Record, and Holdings.* Westport, CT: Greenwood, 1984.
There are no annotations for the 1,164 newspapers and magazines listed. The first Indian newspaper, *The Cherokee Press,* was published in English and Cherokee in Georgia in February 1828. Copies of front pages from fifty periodicals of the early 1980s give a picture of the variety of these publications in the recent period. Many of the titles are included in the microfilm series *American Indian Periodicals,* described below in this section.

Littlefield, Daniel F., and James W. Parins. *American Indian and Alaska Native Newspapers and Periodicals.* 3 vols. Westport, CT: Greenwood, 1984–86.
This well-annotated bibliography covers the period from 1826 to 1985. The annotations indicate the interests and leanings of the publications, and there is a subject index. Lists of titles by type of publication and location and a chronology of titles are also included.

Miller, Sally, ed. *The Ethnic Press in the United States: An Historical Analysis and Handbook.* New York: Greenwood, 1987.
Individual chapters discuss twenty-seven ethnic groups and relate the development and role of their English-language and native-language press to the evolution of the group in the United States.

Simon, Rita J. *Public Opinion and the Immigrant: Print Media Coverage, 1880–1980.* Lexington, MA: D.C. Heath, 1985.
interesting survey of major magazines and some *New York Times* editorials. Although attitudes and changes in attitudes of the journals are documented, no analysis is provided to explain them. Nevertheless, this book would be useful in isolating specific magazines and time periods through which to study attitudes towr.d immigrants.

Locating the Periodicals

Many nineteenth-century U.S. periodicals are now available on microfilm or microfiche. Below are listed several of the larger series which have been compiled by the major publishers of research materials in microform. Although libraries might consider any of these series prohibitively expensive in their entirety, individual titles within each series are available at reasonable cost. Each series has a printed guide which often contains valuable information about the titles included. Cataloging of these materials varies greatly, and interested instructors are cautioned to talk to a reference librarian rather than rely solely on information found in the library catalog.[1]

American Indian Periodicals. Bethesda, MD: University Publications of America. This series is composed of:

> *American Indian Periodicals from the Princeton University Library, 1839–1982.* 129 titles on 2,687 microfiche and 4 reels.
>
> *American Indian Periodicals from the State Historical Society of Wisconsin, 1884–1981.* 41 titles on 13 reels.
>
> *Periodicals by and about American Indians, 1923–1981.* 99 titles on 82 reels.

There is some overlap of titles among the components; all have printed guides, and individual titles are available.

American Periodicals. Over 1,100 titles. Series I: 1741–1800, 33 reels; Series II: 1800–1850, 1,966 reels; Series III: 1850–1900, Civil War and Reconstruction, 771 reels. Ann Arbor, MI: University Microfilms International, 1946–1977.

This is the oldest and most comprehensive of the series, which fortunately was published at a time when libraries were somewhat more liberally funded than they are presently. Thus, the series, or parts of them, are fairly widely available.

Black Journals. 51 titles. Series I: 635 microfiche and 13 reels; Series II: 27 reels. Bethesda, MD: University Publications of America.

Journals in this series were published from 1827 to 1965, with greatest coverage during the late nineteenth- and early twentieth-century period.

Black Newspaper Collection. 19 titles, 1,218 reels. Ann Arbor, MI: UMI Research Collections.

Newspapers from fifteen states published between 1896 and 1988 are included in this set.

Chicano Studies Library Serial Collection. 250 titles, 382 reels. Sunnyvale, CA: Bay Microfilm.

Newspapers from the Chicano Studies Library of the University of California, Berkeley, were filmed for this collection. Covering the period from 1855 to 1990, most of the titles are from the 1950s on; however, there is ample coverage of the first half of the twentieth

century, and over a dozen titles go back to the nineteenth century.
There are a few titles in English; most are in Spanish.

Periodicals on Women and Women's Rights. 24 titles on 29 microfiche and
145 reels. Bethesda, MD: University Publications of America.
Journals published from 1840 to 1936; most are from the early years
of the twentieth century. Coverage of women's magazines of the
nineteenth century is good in the more general *American Periodicals*
series described above.

As with contemporary periodicals, the easiest way to check availability
of specific titles on microform is:

Guide to Microforms in Print. Westport, CT: Microform Review, 1993.
This guide is a comprehensive listing of available material in microform. Volume 1 is an alphabetical listing; volume 2 is a subject
arrangement of the same titles in Dewey decimal number order. The
subject arrangement is extremely broad, which makes browsing
time-consuming but possible.

Indexes to Periodicals

Although many journals can profitably be used for browsing projects,
there are several indexes which could help students narrow their search
for information and attitudes.

Kaiser Index to Black Resources, 1948–1986. 5 vols. Brooklyn, NY:
Carlson Publishing, 1992.
A monumental set covering a vital forty-year period, this index is
derived from a card file maintained by the New York Public Library's
Schomburg Center for Research in Black Culture. Most of the
citations are to articles in 166 magazines, journals, and newspapers,
although some books and pamphlets were also indexed. The Schomburg Center's interlibrary loan department can provide photocopies
of all articles indexed.

Nineteenth Century Readers' Guide to Periodical Literature. 2 vols. New
York: H. W. Wilson, 1944.
Actually compiled in 1944, these two volumes provide the key to
many popular as well as more academic periodicals published from
1880 to 1900, a period rich in its concern for social progress. All the
journals covered by this index are available on microfilm.

Poole's Index to Periodical Literature, 1802–1906. 6 vols. Rev. ed. Reprint. Gloucester, MA: Peter Smith, 1958.

Mr. Poole, a librarian at Yale University, began compiling this index in 1848. Students who use it today need to be told that standard subject headings and consistent subject indexing are twentieth century innovations. This index is by author, title, and key words from the title. Poole's covers a comparatively small number of periodicals which, although not always scholarly, do reflect the interests of a university librarian and not the broad public. Despite these disadvantages, this can be an interesting set to use.

Rose Bibliography (Project). *Analytical Guide and Indexes to the Colored American Magazine, 1909–1960,* 3 vols.; to the *Crisis, 1910–1960,* 3 vols.; and to the *Voice of the Negro, 1904–1907.* Westport, CT: Greenwood, 1974.

Indexes to three of the most widely read African American journals of the period.

8. SELECTED PRIMARY SOURCES: DOCUMENTS, ARCHIVES, AND RESEARCH COLLECTIONS

One-Volume Document Collections

Blassingame, John W., ed. *Slave Testimony: Two Centuries of Letters, Speeches, Interviews, and Autobiographies.* Baton Rouge: Louisiana State University Press, 1977.

An excellent and comprehensive collection of primary sources.

Brotherston, Gordon. *Image of the New World: The American Continent Portrayed in Native Texts.* London: Thames and Hudson, 1979.

This unusual volume is composed of commentaries and translations of Native American Texts from both continents, ranging from pre-Columbian hieroglyphs and pictographs to narratives published in English in the nineteenth century. Although the "translation" of the pictographs on a Toltec screenfold may be too specialized and complex for most undergraduates, the import of a seventeenth-century Algonquin account of whites entering North America is clear.

Busby, Margaret, ed. *Daughters of Africa: An International Anthology of Words and Writings by Women of African Descent from the Ancient Egyptians to the Present.* New York: Pantheon, 1992.

At over one thousand pages, this is a very comprehensive collection.

Ethnic Prejudice in America Series. New York: World Publishing, 1972–74.

Volumes in this series include excerpts from statutes, court cases, government reports, speeches by leading politicians, testimony before Congress, dialogue from movies, articles from newspapers and magazines, and letters and diaries.

McKiernan, Joan, and Robert St. Cyr, eds. *"Mick!"—Anti-Irish Prejudice in America.*

Selzer, Michael, ed. *"Kike!"—Anti-Semitism in America.*

Smith, Elihu, ed. *"Wop!"—Anti-Italian Prejudice in America.*

Wu, Cheng-Tsu, ed. *"Chink!"—A Documentary History of Anti-Chinese Prejudice in America.*

Feldstein, Stanley, and Lawrence Costello. *The Ordeal of Assimilation: A Documentary History of the White Working Class, 1830's to the 1970's.* Garden City, NY: Anchor Press, 1974.

Foner, Philip S., and Daniel Rosenberg. *Racism, Dissent, and Asian Americans from 1850 to the Present: A Documentary History.* Westport, CT: Greenwood, 1993.

This volume provides a welcome alternative to most documentary collections by offering examples of the resistance to prejudice and discrimination rather than just their existence.

Howe, Irving, and Kenneth Libo. *How We Lived: A Documentary History of Immigrant Jews in America, 1880–1930.* New York: R. Marck, 1979.

Locating additional documentary collections. For general collections, use the Library of Congress subject headings MINORITIES--UNITED STATES--HISTORY--SOURCES; for collections limited to a specific group, search [name of the group]--HISTORY--SOURCES.

Archives and Research Collections

The catalogs of the major publishers of microform research collections are overflowing with collections which will be of interest to readers of this book. Since most are expensive, if they are already in the library they were most likely purchased in response to a specialist's need and may not necessarily be cataloged or publicized. It is best to consult with the librarians about collections already in your institution.

The catalogs of the major microform publishers describe each of their collections in great detail. The acquisitions department of the library may have some of these catalogs; if not, publishers are happy to send them. Following are examples of the types of collections available.

1. From University Publications of America (UPA), 4520 East-West Highway, Bethesda, MD, 20814. 800-692-6300.

    American Indian Correspondence: The Presbyterian Historical Society Collection of Missionaries' Letters, 1833–1893. 35 reels.

    The East St. Louis Race Riot of 1917. 8 reels.

    Papers of the US Commission on Wartime Relocation and Internment of Civilians. 35 reels.

    Major Council Meetings of American Indian Tribes. Part I, 13 reels; Part II, 13 reels. Each part covers a different group of tribes. The period covered is 1911–1956.

    Southern Women and Their Families in the 19th Century; Papers and Diaries, 1785–1923. 49 reels.

2. From UMI (University Microfilms International), 300 North Zeeb Road, Ann Arbor, MI, 48106. 800-521-0600.

    Association of Southern Women for the Prevention of Lynching, 1930–1942. 8 reels.

    The BBC Summary of World Broadcasts. 1939–. Updated quarterly. Microfilm and microfiche. Available in various sets and groupings by time period and geographical location.

    The BBC has monitored foreign radio broadcasts from places which are considered of strategic importance, beginning with 5 countries in 1939 and now including 136 countries. The programs are transcribed and translated into English. Due to the volume involved, the film set provides only a representative sample of the material monitored. Scientific and cultural happenings are covered along with political and economic developments. A guide and daily summary of major events in the news accompany the set.

    The Indian Rights Association Papers, 1864–1973. 136 reels.

    The Jane Addams Papers, 1860–1960. 32 reels.

    The correspondence, diaries, speeches, and statements of Jane Addams, along with newspaper and periodical clippings about her, would be invaluable to students studying problems and

achievements of women in the late nineteenth century. The
records and documents related to Hull House and its programs
and problems would lend depth to a study of immigrants and
their assimilation into the society of the United States, as well
as to a study of social-work history.

Pamphlets in American History. 18,589 microfiche.

Published in five groups, with subject-specific sections within
each group.

From Tom Paine's *Common Sense* on, pamphlets have been
important in U.S. history. Often expressing minority viewpoints, they were a fast and efficient way to communicate
opinions and feelings. Of most potential use to readers of this
book are the sections in Group I on Indians (1,519 titles,
mostly from 1825 to 1880) and Women (646 titles, mostly
from the late nineteenth and early twentieth centuries).

3. From other sources

San Francisco-Asiatic Exclusion League Proceedings, 1907–1913.
1 reel. Library Microfilms, 1115 East Arques Ave., Sunnyvale,
CA, 94086.

Tuskegee Institute News Clipping File. 252 reels, in 3 series. Tuskegee, AL: Tuskegee Institute.

A file of newspaper and magazine clippings about Blacks
and events that affected them was maintained at Tuskegee
Institute from 1911 until 1966. Between three hundred
and five hundred newspapers and magazines were
clipped, including major national and southern dailies,
major Black newspapers and several minor ones, and
some special-interest publications. There was an attempt
to cover all sections of the country. Series I is the main
file, arranged by date and subject; Series II is particularly
interesting because of its sections on lynching, towns and
settlements (including information about "Negro towns"),
slavery, emancipation celebrations, theaters, motion pictures, and cartoons. This set is a gold mine of easy-to-read
primary sources. Through articles (and cartoons and editorials) in Black-owned papers, one can hear firsthand
testimony documenting the lives of African Americans in
all parts of the United States.

9. VISUAL SOURCES: FILMS, VIDEOS, PHOTOGRAPHS, AND POSTERS

Films and Videos

Abrash, Barbara, and Catherine Egan, eds. *Mediating History: The MAP Guide to Independent Video by and about African American, Asian American, Latino, and Native American People.* New York: New York University Press, 1992.

A publication of the Media Alternatives Project of New York University's Bobst Library, this is an indispensable guide to understanding, locating, and using video productions independently produced by minority filmmakers. In addition to essays about the use of the films, 126 videos are listed and fully annotated, with subject and chronological indexes to the productions. The chapter on alternative media resources includes lists of film festivals, media arts centers, organizations, journals and newsletters, and distributors. Highly recommended.

Asian American Media Reference Guide: A Catalog of More Than 1000 Asian American Audio-Visual Programs for Rent or Sale in the United States. Edited by Bill J. Gee. New York: Asian CineVision [32 East Broadway, New York NY 10002; 212-925-8685], 1990.

A listing of films from many sources, with rental and purchase prices. Well-annotated with useful indexes by ethnic group and subject.

Educational Film and Video Locator: The Consortium of College and University Media Centers. 2 vols. New York: Bowker, 1990–91.

This catalog of over fifty thousand titles is the basic resource for those desiring to rent educational films and videos at comparatively low cost. The listings, taken from the holdings of a consortium of academic media centers, are annotated and indicate audience level and source for rental. A list of producers and distributors is included.

Film and Video Finder. 3rd ed. 3 vols. Medford, NJ: Plexus, 1991.

Published for the National Information Center for Educational Media, this catalog is one of the most widely used sources for locating films and videos. Over ninety-two thousand fully described titles, including some foreign films. There is a detailed subject index, as well as a list of producers and distributors.

Images of Color: A Guide to Media from and for Asian, Black, Latino, and Native American Communities. New York: Media Network in cooperation with the Center for Third World Organizing [Media Network,

39 West 14th St., Suite 403, New York, NY 10011 212-929-2663], 1987.

A selection of independently produced films, videos, and slide shows "that will provoke thought and discussion." The intended audiences for these productions include community meetings, tenants' associations, and political organizations, as well as classrooms. The 110 titles listed have extensive annotations. The Media Network operates an information center which can offer recommendations on alternative films and videos on more than two hundred topics of social and ethnic concern.

Native American Public Broadcasting Consortium Catalog of Programming. 1994. [P.O. Box 83111, Lincoln, NE 68501; 402-472-3522]
Video programs about Native Americans produced by public broadcasting corporations and independent video producers, including many who are Native American.

Video Sourcebook: A Guide to Approximately 130,000 Programs Currently Available on Video from More Than 2,400 Sources. 15th ed. 2 vols. Detroit: Gale, 1994.
Probably the most comprehensive listing of videos. A subject index and a list of distributors are included.

Weatherford, Elizabeth, and Emelia Seubert, eds. *Native Americans on Film and Television.* New York: Museum of the American Indian. Vol. 1, 1981; vol. 2, 1988.
Catalogs listing approximately six hundred film and video productions about native peoples of the Americas.

Photographs

Photographs surround us, and even those in the daily newspapers and weekly newsmagazines can be used for student projects.

Listed below are examples of the types of works available to aid in designing and undertaking student projects.

Collier, John, Jr., and Malcolm Collier. *Visual Anthropology: Photography as a Research Method.* rev. and exp. ed. Albuquerque: University of New Mexico Press, 1986.
This highly specialized volume might be of interest to instructors looking for insight into the use of photography to study ethnic groups.

Edwards, Elizabeth, ed. *Anthropology and Photography, 1860–1920.* New Haven, CT: Yale University Press, 1992.
> A specialized book based on the premise that we can learn to "read" photographs. Discusses problems of selectivity in the choice of subject for a photograph and also in the collecting policies of museums and other repositories.

Lyman, Christopher M. *The Vanishing Race and Other Illusions: Photographs of Indians by Edward S. Curtis.* Washington, DC: Smithsonian Institution, 1982.
> Curtis was the preeminent photographer of American Indian life from 1900 to 1930, and he published a twenty-volume work of "documentary" photographs. The analysis of some of his works in this volume would be a good way to introduce students to the ways in which a photographer can manipulate costumes, props, poses, and settings in order to convey a message.

Riis, Jacob A. *The Complete Photographic Work of Jacob A. Riis.* Edited by Robert J. Doherty, with an introduction by Ulrich Keiler. New York: Macmillan, 1981. Text-fiche edition.
> Contains all known prints (632) of Riis's photographs on microfiche. Microfiche is useful for classroom display as well as individual study, since many portable microfiche readers can project onto a wall or screen.[2]

Locating additional photographic collections. The Library of Congress uses PHOTOGRAPH to describe actual photographs (not reproductions of photographs). The most efficient way to locate collections of reproductions of photographs is to use the phrase PICTORIAL WORKS in a key word search.

Posters

Posters are a form of popular art with which students are thoroughly familiar. A few sample collections are listed below.

British Posters, 1851–1988, in the Victoria and Albert Museum National Poster Collection. Boston: G. K. Hall, 1990.
> Contains four thousand posters on forty-eight color microfiche, including wartime, advertising, and political works.

Paret, Peter, Beth Irwin Lewis, and Paul Paret. *Persuasive Images: Posters of War and Revolution from the Hoover Institution Archives.* Princeton, NJ: Princeton University Press, 1992.

Color reproductions of more than three hundred posters produced by both sides during World Wars I and II and the period between the wars. The short introduction and individual commentaries on each poster enable the author to re-create the atmosphere during these periods.

United States Documentary Posters from World War II. Washington, DC: Library of Congress, Photoduplication Services, 1978.

Three reels of microfilm contain 1,200 black-and-white images of posters, most of which were issued by government agencies. Offering an extremely instructive view of an earlier period, the human images in these posters are predictably uniform: Japanese are always leering and buck-toothed; Germans are always sinister, glowering, and serious; and Americans are always white and almost always blond.

Locating additional collections of posters. Collections of posters in print and microform can be located in library catalogs by using the Library of Congress subject subdivision POSTERS, as in S = DISCRIMINATION IN EMPLOYMENT--LAW AND LEGISLATION--UNITED STATES-- POSTERS, or by combining the word POSTERS with a specific topic in a key word search, as in K = DISCRIMINATION and POSTERS.

10. SAMPLE SYLLABI

The following sources, described more fully in the annotated bibliography, contain sample syllabi.

Bronstein, Phyllis, and Katheryn Quina, eds. *Teaching a Psychology of People: Resources for Gender and Sociocultural Awareness.*

Butler, Johnnella E., and John C. Walter, eds. *Transforming the Curriculum: Ethnic Studies and Women's Studies.*

Ch'maj, Betty E. M., ed. *Multicultural America: A Resource Book for Teachers of Humanities and American Studies: Syllabi, Essays, Projects, Bibliography.*

Collins, Patricia Hill, and Margaret L. Andersen, eds. *An Inclusive Curriculum: Race, Class, and Gender in Sociological Instruction.*

Dinnerstein, Myra, and Betty Schmitz, eds. *Ideas and Resources for Integrating Women's Studies into the Curriculum.*

Lauter, Paul, ed. *Reconstructing American Literature: Courses, Syllabi, Issues.*

Morgan, Sandra, ed. *Gender and Anthropology: Critical Reviews for Research and Teaching.*

Raby, Rosalind Latiner, ed. *International Master Modules for Internationalizing the Curriculum: A General Catalog.*

Rothschild, Joan. *Teaching Technology from a Feminist Perspective: A Practical Guide.*

Locating additional syllabi. The best source for syllabi in all subject areas is the ERIC database, available either online, on CD-ROM, or as part of the online catalog in every institution which offers a major in education, and in most other colleges. Institutions with an education major are likely to have the documents immediately available on microfiche; if not, they can be purchased easily in either microfiche or print format. Search ERIC using key words describing the subject or course title in which you are interested, and the descriptors HIGHER EDUCATION and SYLLABI, or HIGHER EDUCATION and CURRICULUM DEVELOPMENT.

The library catalog can also be searched using the Library of Congress subject subdivision --OUTLINES, SYLLABI, ETC. after a specific subject heading, as in S = JEWS--HISTORY--OUTLINES, SYLLABI, ETC. or by doing a key word search combining a specific topic with SYLLABI, as in K = CHINESE AMERICANS and SYLLABI.

11. ELECTRONIC COMMUNICATION

Electronic communication via campus and regional networks or through Internet connections can be used to search remote library catalogs and periodical indexes for bibliographical information, to access a broad range of actual documents including government reports and current statistics, and to carry on electronic conversations (and listen in on others' conversations) with people all over the world.

Currently, the most comprehensive directory of Internet sources is:

Braun, Eric. *The Internet Directory.* New York: Fawcett Columbine, 1994. This is an international directory which includes lists of discussion groups, online library catalogs, electronic text resources, electronic journals, online data archives available from many countries, and more. Online addresses are provided for every entry, and there are subscription instructions and some general instructions. This is a directory of resources available and not a discussion of how to use the Internet.

Instructors, students, and researchers wishing to make electronic contact with others in the same field have an overwhelming number of choices. Among the over 1,500 discussion groups described by Braun, the following list is only a small sample of ones which might be of interest to readers of this book. Braun supplies full Internet addresses.[3]

AFAM-L: Discussions of research on African Americans.
> For information: elspaula@mizzoul.bitnet (Paul Roper)

AMWEST-H: Scholarly discussions of nineteenth-century Western American history. Particularly interested in "nontraditional" views, especially those that might illuminate the views of Native Americans.
> To subscribe: listserv@umrvmb.umr.edu

CENTAM-L: Academic discussions regarding Central America.
> For information: michaelb@ksgrsch.harvard.edu (Michael Blackmore)

GC-L: On the global classroom, international student e-mail, and debates.
> For information:chaikim@uriacc.uri.edu

GEOFEM: Discussions of feminism in geography.
> For information: jajone02@ukcc.uky.edu (Jeff Jones)

MCLR-L: the Midwest Consortium for Latino Research.
> For information: 22429bsc@msu.edu (Belinda S. Cook)

MEDFEM-L: Discussion group for topics related to feminism and the Middle Ages.
> For information: jrondeau@oregon.uoregon.edu (Jennifer Rondeau)

MUSLIMS: Academic and nonpolitical education on issues related to Islam and Muslims, including news and book discussions.
> (For information: mughal@alimni.caltech.edu (Asim Mughal)

WORLD-L: About non-Eurocentric world history.
> For information: brown@ccsua.ctstateu.edu (Haines Brown)

XCULT-L: Discussions of intercultural communication.
> For information: oliver@dhvx20.csudh.edu (Oliver Seely)

Instructors looking for the most up-to-date information about Internet resources in specific subject areas might want to gopher to the Clearinghouse for Subject-Oriented Internet Resource Guides at the University of

Michigan. The address is gopher.lib.umich.edu; select "What's New" from the menu.

NOTES

1. For one instructor's description of his own experiences discovering microform materials already in his university library, see T. H. Breen, "Keeping Pace with the Past: Puritans and Planters among the Microforms," *Microform Review* 20 (spring 1991): 60.

2. For an evaluation of several portable microfiche readers for this purpose, see Pat Flowers, "Reference Applications of Color Microfiche: The World in the Palm of Your Hand," *Microform Review* 21 (spring 1992): 65, n. 7.

3. For additional discussions of some of these lists and others, see Patricia S. Kuntz, "African Studies Computer Resources," *College and Research Libraries News* 55 (February 1994): 68–71, which includes a list of African countries with Internet code and connectivity information; Mary Glazier, "Internet Resources for Women's Studies," *College and Research Libraries News* 55 (March 1994): 139–141; and Susana Hinojosa, "Racial and Ethnic Diversity Information Exchange," *College and Research Libraries News* 55 (March 1994): 158, which includes a discussion of the newly created EQUILIBRN bulletin board.

7

Locating Additional Resources: Hints for Searching the Online Catalog

All researchers—especially members of a college faculty—want the books they need located in one place, preferably in their office, but if that is impossible, at least in one area of the library. Alas, the multidisciplinary nature of ethnic studies and multicultural studies dictates that such is not to be. To locate the most relevant monographic and reference material efficiently, one needs to be skillful in utilizing the library's catalog of holdings. Today, even though some still miss the old 3" × 5" cards, the advent of computerized catalogs makes access to library holdings much easier.

BASIC SEARCHING IN THE ONLINE CATALOG

Subject Searching

In subject searching the researcher uses the standardized vocabulary of Library of Congress subject headings.[1] These headings are listed in the "big red books" usually situated near the reference desk or the catalogs. The advantage of this standardized vocabulary is that the terms are defined and applied consistently over time. The problem with standardized headings is that the researcher often does not conceptualize the topic in the same words as the cataloger. Although the Library of Congress does supply "see" references, even these additional headings don't always match the researcher's thinking. Even worse, some catalogs do not contain the "see" references.

Key Word Searching

Because of the complexities and idiosyncrasies of Library of Congress subject headings, many librarians and researchers make use of the online catalog's ability to search by key word. In most online catalog systems a key word search (sometimes called a word search) will look at every word in the author statement, in the title and subtitle, and in the subject headings.

In many cases the most effective search can be constructed by doing a key word search which combines words used in the standard subject headings with one or two other words which more narrowly or clearly define the researcher's interests. Examples of such searches are given later in this chapter.

Boolean Functions—The Use of "and" and "or"

Using "and" between two words or phrases tells the computer to give you only those entries which include *both* words. Thus, if the researcher wants only books on multicultural education written for college instructors, combining the phrases MULTICULTURAL EDUCATION and EDUCATION, HIGHER will eliminate all those books designed for primary and secondary grades.

Using "or" between two words or phrases tells the computer to give you every entry that includes *either* of the words or phrases. Thus, the search WORKING CLASS WOMEN or MINORITY WOMEN will bring a much greater number of entries than would either phrase searched individually.

In general, "and" is recommended when the researcher suspects there is a great deal of information and wants to narrow the search; "or" is recommended when the researcher thinks there are not many entries and wants to see every possibility.

Truncation

Shortening a word to its stem and telling the computer to search all variations—can be used to make key word searches more inclusive and efficient. For example, K = SLAVE? will search SLAVE, SLAVES, and SLAVERY; K = SYLLAB? will search SYLLABI and SYLLABUS (also SYLLABLE and SYLLABLES). Truncation symbols vary with the online system but are most frequently either $ or ?.

MULTICULTURALISM AND LIBRARY OF CONGRESS SUBJECT HEADINGS

Knowing a few general cataloging principles might make understanding the next sections easier.

- Items are always given the most specific subject heading possible. For example, a book of sources about Chinese Americans in U.S. history will be found listed under CHINESE AMERICANS--UNITED STATES--HISTORY--SOURCES, but *not* under MINORITIES--UNITED STATES--HISTORY--SOURCES; a book about Filipino Americans will be found under FILIPINO AMERICANS but *not* under ASIAN AMERICANS.
- Items are given the fewest possible subject headings which can be used to describe their content fully.
- The Library of Congress attempts to use the most appropriate current terminology; changes are made in subject headings to reflect current terminology. However, not every catalog will apply these changes retrospectively.

A Selection of Library of Congress Subject Headings Useful in Multicultural Research

AGE DISCRIMINATION

CROSS CULTURAL ORIENTATION

DISCRIMINATION

EQUAL PAY FOR EQUAL WORK

EQUALITY

ETHNIC ART

ETHNIC ATTITUDES

ETHNIC ATTITUDES IN LITERATURE

ETHNIC RELATIONS

ETHNICITY

ETHNOARCHEOLOGY

ETHNOBOTANY

ETHNOCENTRISM

ETHNOMATHEMATICS

ETHNOPSYCHOLOGY

HOMELESS

INTERCULTURAL COMMUNICATION

INTERCULTURAL EDUCATION

INTERNATIONAL EDUCATION

MINORITIES

MINORITIES AS ARTISTS

MINORITIES--UNITED STATES--BIOGRAPHY

MINORITY WOMEN

MULTICULTURAL EDUCATION

PLURALISM (SOCIAL SCIENCE)

POOR

PREJUDICE

RACE AWARENESS

RACE RELATIONS

RACISM

RACISM IN LANGUAGE

RACISM IN LITERATURE

REVERSE DISCRIMINATION

SEGREGATION

SEGREGATION IN EDUCATION

SEX DISCRIMINATION

SLAVERY

SOCIAL CLASSES

UNITED STATES--EMIGRATION AND IMMIGRATION

WOMEN

WOMEN SLAVES

WOMEN'S STUDIES

WORKING CLASS WOMEN

XENOPHOBIA

In addition to these general headings, the researcher should be aware that the names of specific ethnic, religious, or immigrant groups are also used as subject headings. Works which are limited to a single group will rarely be given a general heading.

Subject Subdivisions

The Library of Congress frequently modifies subject headings, including the names of specific groups, by adding subdivisions to make the subject headings more specific. Below is a list of subdivisions which can be added to almost any subject. Two dashes [--] are usually required between the subdivision and the subject.

--BIOGRAPHY

--CARTOONS, CARICATURES, ETC.

--CROSS-CULTURAL STUDIES

--CULTURAL ASSIMILATION

--CURRICULA

--EDITORIAL CARTOONS

--EDUCATION, HIGHER

--ETHNIC IDENTITY

--ETHNIC RELATIONS

--HISTORY--SOURCES

--OUTLINES, SYLLABI, ETC.

--PERSONAL NARRATIVES

--PICTORIAL WORKS

--PSYCHOLOGICAL ASPECTS

--PSYCHOLOGY

--PUBLIC OPINION

--RACE IDENTITY

--SOCIAL ASPECTS

--STUDY AND TEACHING

Geographic Subdivisions

Names of specific places, where appropriate to define the content of a book narrowly, can also be added, and sometimes will be placed *between* the subject and the subdivision. The researcher who is not interested in geographic distinctions will find that combining the subject and the subdivision in a key word search will increase efficiency and save time.

For example, K = SLAVERY and PERSONAL NARRATIVES will provide all the listings which include personal narratives while saving the researcher the time of looking under each geographic subdivision to see if there is a personal narrative included. The list below illustrates this.

S = SLAVERY--BERMUDA--BIBLIOGRAPHY

S = *SLAVERY--GEORGIA--PERSONAL NARRATIVES*

S = SLAVERY--GREECE--HISTORY

S = SLAVERY--MARYLAND

S = SLAVERY--VIRGINIA--ECONOMIC ASPECTS

S = *SLAVERY--*VIRGINIA--*PERSONAL NARRATIVES*

Subject Headings for Specific Groups[2]

African Americans. This is a complex area because subject headings used to describe this group have changed in response to changes in the terminology accepted as appropriate. For many years, the term used was NEGRO or NEGROES. Today, the Library of Congress has adopted the following practices:

- AFRO-AMERICANS for works about citizens of the United States who are descended from Black Africans.
- BLACKS for works about Blacks outside the United States and about Blacks in the United States who reside here only temporarily. However, works about Black people living in countries whose population is predominantly Black are cataloged under the name of that country. Thus, Black is not used for citizens of Nigeria, but it is used for Black citizens of Sweden.

Both BLACK and AFRO-AMERICAN are also used in hundreds of subdivisions of more general subjects. Following these distinctions is frequently difficult and compounds the intricacy of using the online catalog. The use of both terms in several types of phrase headings further adds to the complexity, as in the following examples:

AFRO-AMERICAN ACTORS

AFRO-AMERICAN AGED

AFRO-AMERICANS IN BUSINESS
AFRO-AMERICANS IN LITERATURE
BLACK BUSINESS ENTERPRISE
BLACK ENGLISH
BLACK RACE
SOCIAL WORK WITH AFRO-AMERICANS

Black is also used in inverted headings, such as:

ACTORS, BLACK
BAPTISTS, BLACK
COLLEGE STUDENTS, BLACK

Afro-American is also used as a subdivision of more general subjects, such as:

AMERICAN FICTION--AFRO-AMERICAN AUTHORS
SERMONS, AMERICAN--AFRO-AMERICAN AUTHORS
UNITED STATES. AIR FORCE--AFRO-AMERICANS

Finally, it should be noted that although many libraries have changed their cataloging for older books from NEGROES to AFRO-AMERI-CANS, many others have not done so because of the costs involved.

Thus, the researcher should do the following:

- Be alert to the period when the book was cataloged and to whether the particular library has updated its older records.

- When doing a key word search and looking for books about residents of the United States, include the Library of Congress terminology (NEGROES or AFRO-AMERICANS or both), even though the use of BLACK and AFRICAN AMERICAN is becoming more frequent today.

- When seeking information about people who may not be considered permanent residents of the United States, include both AFRO-AMERICANS and BLACKS in the key word search.

- Be careful and precise, and expect to spend some time locating the most relevant citations for your work.

Hispanic Americans, Latin Americans, and Chicanos. The Library of Congress offers the following definitions for its headings:

- HISPANIC AMERICANS is used for works on U.S. citizens of Latin American descent. Works dealing with specific groups of Hispanic Americans are entered under the name of the group: CUBAN AMERICANS, CHILEAN AMERICANS, and so forth.
- LATIN AMERICANS--UNITED STATES is used for citizens of Latin America living in the United States. Narrower terms are used for specific groups, such as CUBANS--UNITED STATES and MEXICANS--UNITED STATES.
- CHICANOS is not used as a subject heading. Works about Americans of Mexican heritage are entered under MEXICAN AMERICANS. The word will, of course, occur frequently in title and key word searches.

As with BLACKS and AFRO-AMERICANS, numerous subdivisions are possible for each of the above headings. There are also many phrase headings, including:

HISPANIC AMERICAN BUSINESS ENTERPRISES

TEACHERS OF MEXICAN AMERICANS

CHURCH WORK WITH HISPANIC AMERICANS

MEXICAN AMERICAN CATHOLICS

Headings for literary collections by Hispanic authors are complicated by the two languages as well as some inconsistencies in the treatment of different literary forms. Thus, one finds headings such as:

AMERICAN DRAMA--MEXICAN AMERICAN AUTHORS

MEXICAN AMERICAN DRAMA (SPANISH)

SHORT STORIES, AMERICAN--MEXICAN AMERICAN AUTHORS

Native Americans. Users of catalogs based on the Library of Congress subject headings will find that the following rules apply:

- INDIANS is used for works on aboriginal people of the Western Hemisphere. For convenience, the Library of Congress has divided the hemisphere into five regions: North America, Mexico, Central America, West Indies, and South America.

- Works on the inhabitants of India are entered under EAST INDIANS.
- INDIANS OF NORTH AMERICA refers to Native Americans of the United States and Canada. The name "Native Americans" is not used.
- INDIANS OF MEXICO refers to original people in the area now called Mexico.

Regardless of the region, works limited to a specific tribe will be entered under the name of the tribe rather than under INDIANS OF NORTH AMERICA or INDIANS OF MEXICO. Thus, much valuable information will be found under specific headings such as ABNAKI INDIANS, ATHAPASCAN INDIANS, AZTECS, and ZAPOTEC INDIANS.

Among the useful subdivisions are:

--INDIAN INFLUENCES: usually the third element in a subject heading following the name of a country, such as MEXICO--CIVI-LIZATION--INDIAN INFLUENCES.

--FIRST CONTACT WITH EUROPEANS: usually used after a heading such as INDIANS OF NORTH AMERICA or the name of a specific tribe.

In both cases, using the phrase in a key word search is efficient.

Works on native law can be found under the heading LAW followed by the name of a tribe, such as LAW, CHEROKEE or LAW, CHEYENNE. Works on U.S. laws governing regions or tribes will be found under INDIANS OF NORTH AMERICA--[the name of the state or tribe]--LE-GAL STATUS, LAWS, ETC.

General literary collections by Native Americans follow patterns similar to those for Afro-Americans and Mexican Americans. For example:

AMERICAN FICTION--INDIAN AUTHORS

AMERICAN POETRY--TRANSLATIONS FROM INDIAN LAN-GUAGES

Some works, however, will be given more specific headings such as:

NAVAJO INDIANS--POETRY

Other Groups. Most other groups follow similar patterns:

CHINESE AMERICANS
CHINESE IN THE UNITED STATES
CHINESE--UNITED STATES
AMERICAN POETRY--TRANSLATIONS FROM CHINESE

POLISH AMERICANS
POLES IN THE UNITED STATES
POLES--UNITED STATES
AMERICAN POETRY--POLISH AMERICAN AUTHORS

JEWS--UNITED STATES
JEWS IN THE UNITED STATES
JEWS, AMERICAN (not Jewish Americans), but:
JEWISH JUDGES--UNITED STATES
JEWISH COLLEGE STUDENTS--UNITED STATES
JEWISH FICTION--UNITED STATES
AMERICAN FICTION--JEWISH AUTHORS

NOTES

1. *Library of Congress Subject Headings.* 16th ed. 3 vols. Washington, DC: Library of Congress, 1993.

2. Much of the information in this section is drawn from Lois Olsrud and Jennalyn Chapman Tellman, "Difficulties of Subject Access for Information about Minorities," in Karen Parrish and Bill Katz, eds., *Multicultural Acquisitions* (New York: Haworth Press, 1993), pp. 47–60.

Appendix A

Sample Media Analysis Worksheets
Sample Library Research Worksheets

TELEVISION OBSERVATION WORKSHEET, PART I

Name of program watched; day, date, and time: _____

I. Basic descriptions of the characters.

	Gender	Age	Race	Religion	Ethnic Background	Class
Major characters [list them]						
Minor characters [list them]						
Characters in background and in crowds [describe situation]						

NOTE: Gender and race will usually be clear. Give estimates for age. Religion, class, and ethnic background may emerge from the story, or there may be no way to determine them. Mark each description accordingly (clear, estimate, assume, can't determine).

TELEVISION OBSERVATION WORKSHEET, PART II

II. Personality characteristics.

List each character in the appropriate column, and then choose from the following list of traits to describe each one.

Able to make decisions
Caring
Confident
Follower
Funny—others laugh at

Funny—others laugh with
Generally positive (heroic)
Helps others
Intelligent
Leader

Needs help from others
Silly
Smart and able to do things well
Strong
Stupid and not able to do things well

Troubled; has many problems
Unable to make decisions
Violent
Weak

Men and Boys

Women and Girls

Source: Much of this worksheet is derived from those prepared by Dr. Linda Pershing, State University of New York, at Albany.

SAMPLE RESEARCH WORKSHEET FOR BOOKS

Research topic: _____

1. Search was by: subject heading: _____

                      word or key word: _____

Number of citations found: _____

_____ The search worked well. I found a reasonable number of citations, looked through them all, and listed the most relevant on the back of this sheet.

_____ There were too many citations to go through them all, but I have selected some and listed them on the back.

_____ There were too many citations to go through efficiently. I have tried a different search.

_____ None of the citations located was relevant.

2. Search was by: subject heading: _____

                      word or key word: _____

Number of citations found: _____

_____ The search worked well. I found a reasonable number of citations, looked through them all, and listed the most relevant on the back of this sheet.

_____ There were too many citations to go through them all, but I have selected some and listed them on the back.

_____ There were too many citations to go through efficiently. I have tried a different search.

_____ None of the citations located was relevant.

SAMPLE RESEARCH WORKSHEET FOR ARTICLES

Note: Complete a separate worksheet for each index or database used.

Research topic: _____

Periodical index or database used: _____

Year(s) covered: _____

❖ ❖

List words or subject headings used in searches:

1. _____

The search described above was:

a._____ very useful; right on target.
[List these articles on a separate page]

b._____ possibly useful; a few things which might be helpful.
[List these articles on a separate page]

c._____ not useful because there was nothing there.

d._____ not useful because nothing relevant was found.

e._____ hard to evaluate because too much was found.

2. _____

The search described above was:

a._____ very useful; right on target.
[List these articles on a separate page]

b._____ possibly useful; a few things which might be helpful.
[List these articles on a separate page]

c._____ not useful because there was nothing there.

d._____ not useful because nothing relevant was found.

e._____ hard to evaluate because too much was found.

121

SAMPLE RESEARCH WORKSHEET FOR AN ONLINE CATALOG

NOTE: Some online catalogs contain several databases (for example, the library catalog, *Psychological Abstracts*, *ERIC*, or the Wilson Indexes). This worksheet can be used for all.

I. Database searched:_____

_____

II. Use this section to record subject heading or key word searches which did not yield any significant results. Indicate whether search was by key word or by subject.

III. Use this section to record successful searches.

Use this column to record subject headings or key words used.	Use this column to record author, title, date, and call number of relevant works located.

SAMPLE RESEARCH WORKSHEET FOR REFERENCE BOOKS

Research topic: _____

What information do you need? _____

_____

❖ ❖

1. Reference book consulted: Title, classification, date of publication _____

_____

      I found information which will be very useful on pages _____

      I found information which might be of some use on pages _____

      This book was not useful _____

2. Reference book consulted: Title, classification, date of publication _____

_____

      I found information which will be very useful on pages _____

      I found information which might be of some use on pages _____

      This book was not useful _____

3. Reference book consulted: Title, classification, date of publication _____

_____

      I found information which will be very useful on pages _____

      I found information which might be of some use on pages _____

      This book was not useful _____

Appendix B

Selected List of Small Publishers and Distributors of Multicultural Books

Distributors who can supply books and catalogs from several publishers have been marked with an asterisk (*). Small publishers go out of business more frequently than their mainstream counterparts. All names and numbers on this list were verified in June, 1994.[1]

African Books Collective, Ltd.*
The Jam Factory
27 Park End St.
Oxford, England OX 1 1HU
(44)865-726686; FAX: (44)865-793298
A cooperative distributor of English-language titles from African publishers. Exclusive overseas distributor of works of forty-two publishers from twelve African countries. Catalogs include scholarly, general, and children's books.

Akwe:kon Press
300 Caldwell Hall
Cornell University
Ithaca, NY 14853
Publishes a multidisciplinary scholarly journal of the same name devoted to Native American culture and knowledge, and a small list of original paperback books about Native Americans.

Arte Publico Press
University of Houston
4800 Calhoun
Houston, TX 77204
713-743-2841
Fiction, poetry, drama, literary criticism, and autobiography by Hispanic Americans, with a special focus on women's literature. Publishes *U.S. Hispanic Literary Tradition Series,*

which locates and publishes lost or little-known titles from the eighteenth century to the mid-twentieth century.

Bilingual Review Press
Hispanic Research Center
Arizona State University
Box 872702
Tempe, AZ 85287
602-965-3867
Publishes books by Latinos, and by non-Latinos on Hispanic topics.

Consortium Book Sales & Distribution*
1045 Westgate Drive, Suite 90
St. Paul, MN 55114
612-221-9035; FAX: 612-221-0124
Distributes works from thirty-one small or alternative presses. Extensive catalog lists books by publisher and provides comprehensive author/title and subject indexes. Not limited to multicultural topics, although they are very heavily represented. Includes the publications of Readers International, a British publisher which specializes in English translations of contemporary fiction from all over the world.

Crises Press, Inc.*
1716 SW Williston Rd.
Gainesville, FL 32608
904-335-2200
Distributes works from a large number of alternative publishers. Good source for works about the Third World, social action, and economic issues, as well as ethnic and gender studies.

Curbstone Press
321 Jackson Street
Willimantic, CT 06226
203-423-9190
Latino and Latin American fiction and nonfiction.

The Feminist Press at the City University of New York
311 East 94th Street
New York, NY 10128
212-360-5790; FAX: 212-360-1241
Feminist publications, fiction and nonfiction in all subjects. An early and consistent leader in feminist publishing, with many international titles.

Graywolf Press
2402 University Avenue, Suite 203
St. Paul, MN 55114
612-641-0077; FAX: 612-641-0036
Multicultural works by authors of color. Primarily fiction, including translations.

Heyday Books
2054 University Avenue
Berkeley, CA 94704
510-549-3564
A small list of Native American and California regional topics.

Ian Randle Publishers
206 Old Hope Road
Kingston 6, Jamaica
809-927-2085; FAX: 809-977-0243
Publishes an interesting collection of nonfiction titles about the Caribbean.

Intercultural Press
P.O. Box 700
Yarmouth, ME 04096
207-846-5168; FAX: 207-846-5181
Includes scholarly and popular literature, with a focus on international and cross-cultural understanding. Many business and management titles.

Native American Authors Distribution Project*
Greenfield Review Press
2 Middle Grove Rd., P.O. Box 308
Greenfield Center, NY 12833
518-584-1728; FAX: 518-583-9741
Issues *The North American Native Authors Catalog,* which lists materials from university and trade publishers as well as small presses. Books on all subjects including autobiography, history, sacred traditions, the arts, and fiction. Audiocassettes of music, legends, and poetry. The catalog lists close to four hundred titles from over eighty publishers and includes a unique index by tribal nation as well as by author.

Orbis Books
P.O. Box 308
Maryknoll, NY 10545
800-258-5838
This publisher's mission is "to address the global dimensions of Christianity with special emphasis on the experience and perspective of the poor." Includes works on women's studies, African and Asian studies, and world religions other than Christianity. An interesting selection of titles.

Pandora Book Peddlers: The Multicultural Feminist Bookstore*
885 Belmont Avenue
North Haledon, NJ 07508
201-427-5733

Path Press, Inc.*
53 West Jackson Blvd., Suite 724
Chicago, IL 60604
312-663-0167
Publishes a catalog called *Pathways: A Minority Press Review: A Comprehensive Guide to Titles by Minority Authors and Publishers.* The primary focus of this distributor is on books about African Americans, although there are some listings about other minority groups and about women. Titles are from mainstream and alternative presses, and most are annotated.

The Small Press Center*
20 West 44th Street
New York, NY 10036
212-764-7021
The New York City office of this small-press distributor has a reference center where many of the books—including multicultural titles—are on display.

Small Press Distribution, Inc.*
1814 San Pablo Avenue
Berkeley, CA 94702
510-549-3336; FAX: 510-544-2201
Titles from over three hundred independent presses with emphasis on "contemporary literary arts." Publishes an extensive, but unannotated, catalog arranged by author and title, but with indexes which facilitate identification of multicultural titles.

South End Press Collective
116 Saint Botolph Street
Boston, MA 02115
800-533-8578
Publications on feminism, grassroots democracy, antiracism, multiculturalism, and international solidarity.

Wasatch Book Distribution*
Box 117776
Salt Lake City, UT 84147
801-575-6735; FAX: 801-521-8243
Distributes books of more than 150 publishers on a variety of subjects. Includes a good selection of works about Native Americans.

Weatherhill*
420 Madison Avenue
New York, NY 10017
212-223-3008; FAX: 212-223-2584
This publisher of books about Asia is also a distributor of English-language books on Asia and the Pacific produced by other companies. Titles listed in the catalog have been published in Asia and Africa as well as in the United States. Books on all subjects; some translations. Fiction and poetry as well as nonfiction.

Instructors seeking additional sources of ethnic publications should look at the lists in the Gale Information Directories. Those looking for additional sources of non-U.S. materials may want to consult *International Literary Market Place* and *Willings Press Guide*. All are discussed more fully in Chapter 6.

NOTE

1. Names of a number of the publishers and distributors were taken originally from a list prepared by Carol F. L. Liu of Queensborough Public Library for a meeting of the Ethnic Studies Round Table of the New York Library Association. Ms. Liu's list was brought to my attention by Prof. David Cohen, Queens College School of Library and Information Science.

Selected
Annotated Bibliography

Recent academic and public interest in multicultural research and education has resulted in what appears to the researcher to be an endless number of reference books, monographs, essays, and articles on the subject. It is now at the point where, if one would attempt to read all that is available—or even a significant portion—one would never get around to acting on what one has read.

The list below is a personal selection which should be both useful and interesting to readers of this book. In the belief that the teaching experiences of faculty in one discipline can be of benefit to those in other disciplines, and in the hope that readers of this book will browse through the entire list for sources of ideas as well as information, this bibliography is arranged alphabetically rather than by subject. Titles annotated in Chapter 6 are not repeated here, but are included in the author/title index.

Acuna, Rodolfo. *Occupied America: A History of Chicanos.* 3rd ed. New York: Harper & Row, 1988.
> Starting with the early nineteenth century, this volume presents a comprehensive history. Each chapter begins with a helpful overview.

Adams, J. Q., James F. Niss, and Cynthia Suarez, eds. *Multicultural Education: Strategies for Implementation in Colleges and Universities.* Macomb: Western Illinois University, 1991. ERIC document ED 346 811.
> Programs in a number of different subject areas are described.

Aerni, April Laskey. "Using Feminist Pedagogy in the Economics Classroom." Unpublished paper presented at the New Jersey Project Conference, "The Inclusive Curriculum: Setting Our Own Agenda," Parsippany, NJ, April 1993.
> Professor Aerni, from Nazareth College of Rochester, describes several changes in content and major changes in her teaching style. Her paper includes a good bibliography.

Allen, Irving Lewis. *Unkind Words: Ethnic Labeling from Redskin to WASP.* New York: Bergin & Garvey, 1990.
> A discussion of the older, traditional ethnic slurs is followed by one dealing with

the "newer devices," including euphemisms, mispronunciations, and codewords. Good bibliography.

Altbach, Philip G., and Gail P. Kelly, eds. *Textbooks in the Third World: Policy, Content, and Context.* New York: Garland, 1988.

An interesting book of readings which would be useful in education courses. Articles discuss aspects of textbooks and textbook publishing in Iran, India, Nigeria, Malaysia, and Indochina and describe the problems of many textbooks in those countries still reflecting the interests of the colonial powers.

American Council on Education. *Minorities on Campus: A Handbook for Enhancing Diversity.* Edited by Madeleine F. Green. Washington, DC, 1989.

A short handbook discussing all aspects of minorities on campus, including recruiting and retaining students, administrators, and faculty, as well as problems of teaching, learning, and the curriculum. Checklists and many practical suggestions are included, and there are brief descriptions of effective programs with addresses and phone numbers.

———. *Sources: Diversity Initiatives in Higher Education: A Directory of Programs, Projects, and Services for African Americans, Asian Americans, Hispanic Americans, and Native Americans in Higher Education.* Washington, DC, 1993.

More than two hundred associations, organizations, and programs in over eight hundred colleges and universities and hundreds of state and federal agencies are listed and annotated. Concerned with all aspects of multiculturalism on campus: recruitment, retention, student services, faculty development, and curriculum.

Anderson, James A. "Theme: Minorities; Cognitive Styles and Multicultural Populations." *Journal of Teacher Education* 39 (January-February 1988): 2–9.

An excellent summary of the topic, cited by many others in the field. Useful charts and an extensive bibliography (through 1985).

Bailey, Frankie Y. *Out of the Woodpile: Black Characters in Crime and Detective Fiction.* Westport, CT: Greenwood, 1991.

An interesting example of the highly specialized studies now being done.

Baird, Robert M., and Stuart E. Rosenbaum. *Bigotry, Prejudice, and Hatred: Definitions, Causes, and Solutions.* Buffalo, NY: Prometheus Books, 1992.

This well-written study starts with discussions of hatred and prejudice from traditional (Abraham Kaplan), classic (Gordon Allport), and revisionist (Paula Rothenberg) points of view, and then provides descriptions of the problems and attempted solutions on specific campuses.

Banks, James A. *Teaching Strategies for Ethnic Studies.* 5th ed. Boston: Allyn and Bacon, 1991.

Although written as a textbook for teachers in primary and secondary grades, this widely cited standard work will prove equally valuable to college instructors. Comprehensive overviews of several ethnic groups, chronologies, study questions, exercises, and unusually well selected and annotated bibliographies are included.

Battle, Dolores E., ed. *Communication Disorders in Multicultural Populations.* Boston: Andover Medical Publishers, 1993.

This compilation is an example of the highly specialized works now available to those interested in the full range of implications of our multicultural world. Although addressed primarily to speech pathologists and audiologists, it has much wider implications, especially for instructors in multicultural situations.

Black Women in America: An Historical Encyclopedia. 16 vols. Brooklyn, NY: Carlson, 1993.

Not really an encyclopedia, this is an ambitious undertaking containing a collection of previously published articles in a chronological and topical arrangement.

Border, Laura L. B., and Nancy Van Note Chism, eds. *Teaching for Diversity.* San Francisco: Jossey-Bass, 1992.

One of the more readable and useful collections devoted to pedagogy in the college environment. Individual essays include discussions of cultural inclusion, learning styles, issues related to women students, and faculty development programs. Annotated bibliographies. *Highly recommended.*

Brett, Guy. *Through Our Own Eyes: Popular Art and Modern History.* Philadelphia: New Society Publishers, 1987.

Interesting and perceptive descriptions of contemporary popular art from China, Chile, and Africa.

Brislin, Richard W., ed. *Applied Cross-Cultural Psychology.* Newbury Park, CA: Sage, 1990.

A comprehensive overview of the subject.

Bronstein, Phyllis, and Katheryn Quina, eds. *Teaching a Psychology of People: Resources for Gender and Sociocultural Awareness.* Washington, DC: American Psychological Association, 1988.

Essential for those teaching psychology, this work will also be of interest to those in other disciplines looking for examples of the way in which multiculturalism can be incorporated into traditional lower-division courses. "Resources, perspectives, and techniques to guide and support instructors in developing approaches suitable for their own courses" are discussed, with particularly interesting descriptions of integrating introductory-level classes. Specific syllabi are examined, and there are excellent bibliographies. *Highly recommended.*

Buenker, John D., and Lorman A. Ratner, eds. *Multiculturalism in the United States: A Comparative Guide to Acculturation and Ethnicity.* Westport, CT: Greenwood, 1992.

This book would be an excellent starting point from which to accumulate information about the ten ethnic groups which are covered. History of emigration, the nature and extent of assimilation, and roadblocks to assimilation are among the topics covered. There is an extensive annotated bibliography for each chapter in addition to a bibliographic essay.

Butler, Johnnella E., and John C. Walter, eds. *Transforming the Curriculum: Ethnic Studies and Women's Studies.* Albany: State University of New York Press, 1991.

Several well-known authors are among the contributors of chapters describing the teaching of courses in African American history and women studies. Course outlines and bibliographies are included.

Buttjes, Dieter, and Michael Byram, eds. *Mediating Languages and Cultures: Towards an Intercultural Theory of Foreign Language Education.* Clevedon, Avon, England: Multilingual Matters, 1991.

Articles in this book are concerned with attempts within Europe to achieve intercultural education within the context of foreign-language teaching. Various programs, approaches and problems are addressed.

Calloway, Colin G., ed. *New Directions in American Indian History.* Norman: University of Oklahoma Press, 1988.
This volume of excellent, evaluative, bibliographic essays covering areas including economics, religion, role of women, population, language, law, and the application of quantitative methods would be a good first place to look for scholarly books and articles on Native Americans.

Cannon, Lynn Weber. "Fostering Positive Race, Class, and Gender Dynamics in the Classroom." *Women's Studies Quarterly* 18 (1990): 126–134. Reprinted in Patricia Hill Collins and Margaret L. Andersen, eds., *An Inclusive Curriculum: Race, Class, and Gender in Sociological Instruction* (Washington, DC: American Sociological Association, 1987).
This influential and frequently cited article lists ground rules and objectives for a positive and productive multicultural classroom environment.

Capek, Mary Ellen S. *A Women's Thesaurus: An Index of Language Used to Describe and Locate Information by and about Women.* New York: Harper & Row, 1987.
A thesaurus including lists of related terms and broader and narrower terms. The value of this work is not limited to women studies, but extends to those interested in almost any aspect of language in relation to diversity.

Ch'maj, Betty E. M., ed. *Multicultural America: A Resource Book for Teachers of Humanities and American Studies: Syllabi, Essays, Projects, Bibliography.* Lanham, MD: University Press of America, 1993.
Syllabi from specialized and mainstream courses, a variety of insightful essays, bibliographies, a videography, and a list of multicultural fictional favorites make this book one of the most valuable available. *Highly recommended.*

Clark, Katherine W. "Using Multi-Ethnic Literature in the Composition Classroom: Overcoming the Obstacles." Paper presented at the Annual Conference of the Society for the Study of the Multi-Ethnic Literature of the United States, Irvine, CA, April, 1987. ERIC document ED 291 847.
Obstacles discussed include student resistance, large classes, resistance by other members of the department, reluctance of recent immigrants to study their own culture, and the paucity of appropriate textbooks.

Collins, Patricia Hill, and Margaret L. Andersen, eds. *An Inclusive Curriculum: Race, Class, and Gender in Sociological Instruction.* Washington, DC: American Sociological Association, 1987.
The overview essays, discussions of teaching strategies, and bibliographies make this an extremely useful book. Included are sixteen syllabi from traditional sociology courses, as well as five from courses specifically devoted to race, class, and gender.

Cordasco, Francesco. *The Immigrant Woman in North America: An Annotated Bibliography of Selected References.* Metuchen, NJ: Scarecrow, 1985.
Informative abstracts arranged by broad subjects, with an index including references to specific immigrant groups, make this small volume still worthwhile despite its age.

Crawley, Donna, and Martha Ecker. "Integrating Issues of Gender, Race, and Ethnicity into Experimental Psychology and Other Social-Science Methodology Courses." *Women's Studies Quarterly* 18, nos. 1, 2 (1990): 105–116.

Practical advice and specific descriptions for those teaching social science methodology courses.

Danahay, Martin A. "Breaking the Silence: Symbolic Violence and the Teaching of Contemporary 'Ethnic' Autobiography." *College Literature* 18 (October 1991): 64–79.

An analysis of violence in autobiographical works by Angelou, Kingston, and Rodriguez, and a discussion of the ways in which such texts can be used within the college and the curriculum.

Davis, Nancy J. "Teaching about Inequality: Student Resistance, Paralysis, and Rage." *Teaching Sociology* 20 (July 1992): 232–238.

In this article, a description of types of student reactions is followed by a discussion of specific projects and strategies (including simulation games, films, and music) utilized to overcome difficulties encountered when teaching a course on social stratification.

Demarest, David P. *"The River Ran Red": Homestead 1892.* Pittsburgh: University of Pittsburgh Press, 1992.

A short, illustrated volume of excerpts from contemporary press preceded by a good introduction, this volume could be used as a sample for students compiling an anthology of primary sources.

Dinnerstein, Leonard, Roger L. Nichols, and David M. Reimers. *Natives and Strangers: Blacks, Indians, and Immigrants in America.* 2nd ed. New York: Oxford University Press, 1990.

A well-done survey providing an integrated chronological history, rather than presenting each group separately.

Dinnerstein, Myra, and Betty Schmitz, eds. *Ideas and Resources for Integrating Women's Studies into the Curriculum.* 2 vols. Tucson: University of Arizona Press, 1986.

Volume 2 is composed of sample syllabi from frequently taught mainstream courses (not women studies courses) which consider issues related to race and ethnicity as well as to women.

Dorn, Dean S. "Simulation Games: One More Tool on the Pedagogical Shelf." *Teaching Sociology* 17 (January 1989): 1–18.

This is an extremely thorough overview of the key features, value, effectiveness, proper use, and problems involved with using simulations in the classroom. An extensive literature review and bibliography and descriptions of thirteen games frequently used in teaching sociology are included.

Dorwith, Vicky E., and Marie Henry. "Optical Illusions: The Visual Representation of Blacks and Women in Introductory Criminal Justice Textbooks." *Journal of Criminal Justice Education* 3 (fall 1992): 251–260.

A careful content analysis is given of the photographs and that analysis is then discussed in terms of the actual numbers of women and Blacks involved with the criminal justice system in positions of authority, as victims, and as offenders. This entire issue of the journal is devoted to women and criminal justice.

Duffee, David E., and Frankie Y. Bailey. "A Criminal Justice Contribution to a General Education Diversity Requirement." *Journal of Criminal Justice Education* 2 (spring 1991): 141–157.

An excellent article describing a first attempt to make a traditional course a vehicle for diversity. Successes, problems, and failures are described; and there are a list of student readings, an excellent bibliography, and a list of works recommended for an instructor intending to teach a similar course.

Fernandez, John P. *The Diversity Advantage: How American Business Can Out-Perform Japanese and European Companies in the Global Marketplace.* New York: Lexington Books, 1993.

A popularly written book which might be effective in stimulating thinking about diversity in introductory business and economics classes. Interesting chapters on women in Japan and ethnocentrism and racism in Japan and European countries.

Flowers, Pat. "Reference Applications of Color Microfiche: The World in the Palm of Your Hand." *Microform Review* 21 (spring 1992): 62–66.

Review of a number of collections of color microfiche with a discussion of methods for using them in the classroom.

Foner, Philip S., and Daniel Rosenberg. *Racism, Dissent, and Asian Americans from 1850 to the Present: A Documentary History.* Westport, CT: Greenwood, 1993.

An extremely thoughtful and unusual approach to a document collection, this volume illustrates the complexities of history by focusing on the dissent from policies and prejudices. Documents include excerpts from laws, sermons, letters, editorials, resolutions, speeches, articles, and pamphlets. Among the well-known authors included are Mark Twain, Henry George, Wendell Phillips, Victoria Woodhull, and Frederick Douglass. The introduction provides a useful overview of dissent from anti-Asian racism and a brief review of the scholarly literature on the subject.

Frey, Raymond. "Can a White Professor Teach African-American History? A Personal Perspective." *Transformations* 4 (spring 1993): 45–49.

Fuhrmann, Barbara Schneider, and Anthony F. Grasha. *A Practical Handbook for College Teachers.* Boston: Little, Brown, 1983.

This frequently cited work will be helpful for those interested in theories of learning styles and their relationship to teaching techniques.

Gates, Henry Louis, Jr. *The Signifying Monkey: A Theory of Afro-American Literary Criticism.* New York: Oxford University Press, 1988.

Instructors first contemplating the introduction of African or African American literature into their courses may want to look at this short, thought-provoking work.

Grant, Carl A., ed. *Research and Multicultural Education: From the Margins to the Mainstream.* London: Falmer Press, 1992. Professors of education in U.S. universities are the major contributors to this book, which is concerned with the education of potential teachers of levels from primary school to college. The articles are research-oriented and scholarly, and contain excellent bibliographies.

Hapke, Laura. *Tales of the Working Girl: Wage-Earning Women in American Literature, 1890–1925.* New York: Twayne Publishers, 1992.

A scholarly study whose bibliographies of the relevant fiction, essays, and literary criticism of the period should prove a practical source for those looking for undergraduate projects in this area.

Higginbotham, Elizabeth. "Designing an Inclusive Curriculum: Bringing All Women into the Core." *Women's Studies Quarterly* 18 (1990): 7–23.

This article includes a good theoretical introduction, as well as a description of the problems encountered and some practical suggestions for meeting them. The focus includes racial minorities as well as women.

Hine, Darlene Clark, ed. *The State of Afro-American History: Past, Present, and Future.* With an introduction by Thomas C. Holt. Baton Rouge: Louisiana State University Press, 1986.

An excellent book containing chapters on various aspects of African American history and discussions of how it is currently being taught.

Hirschfelder, Arlene B., Mary Gloyne Byler, and Michael A. Dorris. *Guide to Research on North American Indians.* Chicago: American Library Association, 1983.

Detailed annotations and useful introductions to each subject area make this book a good starting point for research despite its age.

Jaimes, M. Annette, ed. *The State of Native America: Genocide, Colonization, and Resistance.* Boston: South End Press, 1992.

This thought-provoking series of essays represents the ideas of some of the more outspoken contemporary theorists of Native American history. The valuable table of key laws and court cases about Native Americans that is included could be useful in designing student research projects.

Jones, Jacqueline. *Labor of Love, Labor of Sorrow: Black Women, Work, and the Family from Slavery to the Present.* New York: Basic Books, 1985.

Well-written and thoroughly documented, this study is considered by many to be the basic work in the field.

Karp, Ivan, and Steven D. Lavine, eds. *The Poetics and Politics of Museum Display.* Washington, DC: Smithsonian Institution Press, 1991.

A very readable series of essays which might be valuable in devising innovative student projects. The book's focus includes history and ethnography museums as well as art museums, and its concerns are with curatorial, educational, and public relations issues.

Kivisto, Peter, and Dag Blanck, eds. *American Immigrants and Their Generations: Studies and Commentaries on the Hansen Thesis after Fifty Years.* Urbana: University of Illinois Press, 1990.

The thoughtful, well-researched essays in this volume would be good source ideas for student research topics. Included are essays on the historical novel as collective history, folk dancing and music among the second generation, and ethnicity and the problem of generations.

Kramarae, Cheris, and Dale Spender, eds. *The Knowledge Explosion: Generations of Feminist Scholarship.* New York: Teachers College Press, 1992.

Thorough and substantial assessments of the history, current status, problems, and future direction of feminist scholarship. Forty-four separate essays cover almost every conceivable academic discipline in the sciences, social sciences, humanities, and the professions. Each essay includes a substantial bibliography and literature review. *Highly recommended.*

Lauter, Paul, ed. *Reconstructing American Literature: Courses, Syllabi, Issues.* New York: Feminist Press, 1983.

Syllabi from sixty-seven different American literature courses ranging from single-term introductory courses to advanced upper-level thematic courses are provided. Diversity, changing esthetic standards, and the nature of standard anthologies are discussed in the introduction to this valuable volume.

Levine, Lawrence W. "Clio, Canons, and Culture." *Journal of American History* 88 (December 1993): 849–867.

The presidential address to the Organization of American Historians, this article is a cogent and thoroughly documented defense of the new history and an attack on those who decry "political correctness." By briefly summarizing the history of curriculum reform in the United States, Levine puts the new emphasis on ethnic and social history into perspective.

Lewis, Chris H. *Developing an Inclusive Curriculum: A Curriculum Guide for Multicultural Education.* Minneapolis: General College, University of Minnesota, 1990. ERIC document ED 326 089.

A 268-page bibliography compiled as a working document by the faculty of the General College of the University of Minnesota. An introductory section is followed by lists of resources for multicultural teaching in specific disciplines. Attempts have been made to provide sources of information related to race, ethnicity, gender, and power for each discipline. The depth of coverage varies; some bibliographies are annotated.

Lim, Shirley Geok-lin, and Amy Ling, eds. *Reading the Literatures of Asian America.* Philadelphia: Temple University Press, 1992.

A pioneering book of essays concerned with questions of identity, race, gender, and history and criticism of literary work by Asian Americans. Opening up the issue of diversity within the Asian American community, this book includes extensive but unannotated bibliographies.

Limerick, Patricia Nelson. *The Legacy of Conquest: The Unbroken Past of the American West.* New York: W. W. Norton, 1987.

A pioneering and extremely readable reinterpretation of the American West, this work is one of the first attempts to look at events from the point of view of each of the participants. *Highly recommended.*

Lippard, Lucy R. *Mixed Blessings: New Art in a Multicultural America.* New York: Pantheon, 1990.

This is a valuable study which discusses work currently being done by minority artists. There are many illustrations and an excellent bibliography.

Maggio, Rosalie. *The Dictionary of Bias-free Usage: A Guide to Nondiscriminatory Language.* Phoenix, AZ: Oryx, 1991.

This very useful handbook includes a dictionary listing biased words (with alternatives) and a set of writing guidelines which point out some of the problems involved in attempts to achieve bias-free language.

Marquez, Benjamin. *LULAC: The Evolution of a Mexican American Political Organization.* Austin: University of Texas Press, 1993.

Numerous practical ideas for student projects will come to mind while reading this book.

Martin, Patricia Preciado. *Songs My Mother Sang to Me: An Oral History of Mexican American Women.* Tucson: University of Arizona Press, 1992.

The stories of the ten women from rural and urban Arizona which are contained in this book could be a helpful way to demonstrate oral history as a source of information. Most of the women were born early in this century; themes covered include family and community life, religious practices, gender roles, community building, and cultural resiliency.

Meyers, Chet, and Thomas B. Jones. *Promoting Active Learning: Strategies for the College Classroom.* San Francisco: Jossey-Bass, 1993.

One of the best works on the subject of active learning, this book contains numerous practical examples and hints on strategies for active learning. Well-grounded in earlier theoretical and practical research, it is thoroughly documented and includes an excellent bibliography. *Highly recommended.*

Mindel, Charles H., Robert W. Habenstein, and Roosevelt Wright, Jr. *Ethnic Families in America: Patterns and Variations.* 3rd ed. New York: Elsevier, 1988.

The focus of this volume includes "socioreligious" minorities such as Amish, Muslims, and Mormons, as well as European, Asian, and Hispanic ethnic minorities. Family structure, cultural values, and life cycle attitudes are among the areas studied for each group.

Monastersky, Richard. "The Warped World of Mental Maps: Students Worldwide Share a Skewed Vision of the Continents." *Science News* 142 (October 3, 1992): 222–223.

A brief article which includes a description of an experiment which asked college students from twenty cities around the world to draw a map of the world. As expected, most students gave an undue prominence to their own country or region; what was unexpected was that students from every country "greatly enlarged the size of Europe and shrank the dimensions of Africa."

Morgan, Sandra, ed. *Gender and Anthropology: Critical Reviews for Research and Teaching.* Washington, DC: American Anthropological Association, 1989.

Intended to help instructors of undergraduate anthropology courses incorporate the new research on women into their courses, this model volume will also prove helpful to those teaching in allied areas. Scholarly and well-documented introductory essays are followed by sample syllabi which include annotated bibliographies, film and video listings, and many useful exercises and student projects. As with many of the best recent books in women studies, there is a concern for issues of race and class as well as of gender.

Nochlin, Linda. "Why Have There Been No Great Women Artists?" *Art News* 69 (January 1971): 22–39, 67–71. Reprinted in Thomas Hess and Elizabeth Baker, eds., *Art and Sexual Politics* (New York: Macmillan, 1973).

An early and influential contribution to the discussion of women in art.

Ognibene, Elaine R. "Integrating the Curriculum: From Impossible to Possible." *College Teaching* 37 (summer 1989): 105–110.

A thoughtful article describing both successes and specific problems in attempts at integrating the curriculum in a small college.

Pearson, Carol S., Donna L. Shavlik, and Judith G. Touchton, eds. *Educating the Majority: Women Challenge Tradition in Higher Education.* New York: American Council on Education and Macmillan Publishing, 1989.

The twenty-nine specialized chapters of this book, together with the section introductions, probably represent as thorough and scholarly a discussion of higher education for women as one can find. Excellent bibliographies note the seminal works in each area.

Peters, Arno. *Die Neue Kartographie/The New Cartography.* New York: Friendship Press, 1983.

This is a scholarly discussion of the history, politics, and techniques of mapmaking; text is in German and English.

————. *Peters Atlas of the World.* New York: Harper & Row, 1990.

An extremely illuminating atlas. Highlights include the world in forty-three maps drawn to the same scale, world maps with the equator in the center, and thematic maps which include religion, health, language, and economics. Not widely available, but worth an effort to locate.

Raby, Rosalind Latiner, ed. *International Master Modules for Internationalizing the Curriculum: A General Catalog.* 1991. ERIC document ED 336 150.

Produced by the Institute for International Programs at Los Angeles Community College, this work is a catalog of over 175 courses in sixty different disciplines which have been given an international component or approach.

Rosser, Sue V. *Female-Friendly Science: Applying Women's Studies Methods and Theories to Attract Students.* New York: Pergamon, 1990.

The first few chapters of this work contain a good summary of the highlights of feminist pedagogical thinking; the remainder of the book applies those theories to teaching science. Extensive bibliography.

Rothenberg, Paula. "Teaching 'Racism and Sexism in a Changing America.' " *Radical Teacher* 27 (1984): 2–5.

The experiences in classroom management and pedagogy described in this discussion of a specialized class team-taught by a member of the women studies department and a member of the Afro-American studies department could prove helpful to those teaching in more traditional disciplines.

Rothenberg, Paula, ed. *Race, Class, and Gender in the United States: An Integrated Study.* 2nd ed. New York: St. Martin's, 1992.

Among the best books of readings, this volume includes essays considering the issue of class as well as those of race and gender.

Rothschild, Joan. *Teaching Technology from a Feminist Perspective: A Practical Guide.* New York: Pergamon, 1988.

A practical book containing a useful discussion of the problems, followed by sample syllabi (mostly from upper-division courses) and good bibliographies.

Sadker, Myra, and David Sadker. "Confronting Sexism in the College Classroom." In Susan L. Gabriel and Isaiah Smithson, eds., *Gender in the Classroom: Power and Pedagogy.* Urbana: University of Illinois Press, 1990.

A discussion of sexism in language by two of the leading researchers in the field.

Sanders, Rickie. "Integrating Race and Ethnicity into Geographic Gender Studies." *Professional Geographer* 42 (1990): 228–231.

The author points out the need for the profession to incorporate race and feminist studies into geographical studies. Excellent short bibliography.

Scott, Anne Firor. *Natural Allies: Women's Associations in American History.* Urbana: University of Illinois Press, 1991.

An extremely well done study which discusses the importance of these associations in earlier periods of American history and maintains that they were so successful because talented women had no other outlets for their talents. This book will be valuable in designing student projects relating to women. *Highly recommended.*

Scott, Robert A. "Campus Developments in Response to the Challenges of Internationalization: The Case of Ramapo College of New Jersey." Speech presented at the Organization for Economic Cooperation and Development, General Conference,

Programme on Institutional Management in Higher Education, Paris, September 1992. ERIC document ED 345 678.

Shan, Sharan-Jeet, and Peter Bailey. *Multiple Factors: Classroom Mathematics for Equality and Justice.* Stoke-on-Trent, Staffordshire, England: Trentham Books, 1991.

A handbook describing methods and strategies for multicultural and antiracist mathematics written for secondary school teachers in England.

Spanier, Bonnie. "Encountering the Biological Sciences: Ideology, Language, and Learning." In Anne Herrington and Charles Moran, eds., *Writing, Teaching, and Learning in the Disciplines.* New York: Modern Language Association of America, 1992.

This essay is a thoughtful feminist analysis of the ideologies and practices inherent in traditional microbiology and in its teaching. The new social studies of science and efforts to reconcile differences between education in the sciences and that in the humanities and social sciences are also discussed.

Spradley, James P. *The Ethnographic Interview.* New York: Holt, Rinehart and Winston, 1979.

This is a book designed to give guidance to students and professionals who want to do ethnographic studies but who do not have long years of training in anthropology. It is specifically directed to urban situations rather than "exotic" field experience.

Spradley, James P., and David W. McCurdy. *The Cultural Experience: Ethnography in a Complex Society.* Chicago: Science Research Associates, 1972.

A clear, readable explanation of how to do urban ethnographies, written for undergraduate students and their instructors. The twelve student-written ethnographies include studies of an urban jewelry store, a senior citizen residence, fire fighters, and several levels of schools.

Stannard, David E. *American Holocaust: Columbus and the Conquest of the New World.* New York: Oxford University Press, 1992.

Thoughtful, erudite, broad-ranging, extremely well written study focusing on Indians of both North and South America. *Highly recommended.*

Stross, Randall E. *Bulls in the China Shop: and Other Sino-American Business Encounters.* New York: Pantheon, 1990.

This popularly written work discusses some of the problems encountered by people from the United States when they attempt to work within the international community.

Takaki, Ronald. *A Different Mirror: A History of Multicultural America.* Boston: Little, Brown, 1993.

A long-awaited volume by a leading historian of multicultural America, this book is a narrative history with diverse populations integrated into the story. *Highly recommended.*

———. *Strangers from a Different Shore: A History of Asian Americans.* Boston: Little, Brown, 1989.

Considered one of the best general histories of the subject, this book is scholarly and well written.

Takaki, Ronald, ed. *From Different Shores: Perspectives on Race and Ethnicity in America.* New York: Oxford University Press, 1987.

A justifiably popular anthology of articles on multicultural America. Divided into sections labeled "culture," "class," "gender," and "prospects," the essays are extremely readable and cover a wide variety of groups and problems.

Tanur, Judith M., ed. *Questions about Questions: Inquiries into the Cognitive Bases of Surveys*. New York: Russell Sage Foundation, 1992.
Highly specialized, but thought provoking and readable, this work will be useful for instructors who want to introduce students to the concept of questioning the questions.

Thompson, Becky, and Estelle Disch. "Feminist, Anti-racist, Anti-oppression Teaching: Two White Women's Experience." *Radical Teacher* 41 (spring 1992): 4–14.
The authors analyze their experiences in attempting to teach antiracist and feminist viewpoints in courses in sociology, women studies, and social psychology to both racially mixed and homogeneous classes. Concerned with both course content and classroom processes, the article includes worthwhile discussions of the use of cooperative learning styles and of ways to deal with resistance in the classroom.

Trenton, Patricia, and Patrick T. Houlihan. *Native Americans: Five Centuries of Changing Images*. New York: Harry N. Abrams, 1989.
Written by an art historian and an anthropologist, this volume discusses artists' representations of Native Americans in terms of anthropological and historical accuracy. The book is arranged by Native American cultural group and covers the period from the first representations until the mid-twentieth century.

Whitten, Lisa. "Managing Student Reactions to Controversial Issues in the College Classroom." *Transformations* 4 (spring 1993): 30–44.
This article may be useful for instructors encountering problems arising from attempts to introduce multiculturalism.

Wolfgang, Aaron. "The Silent Language in the Multicultural Classroom." *Theory into Practice* 16 (1977): 145–152.
An excellent summary of the problems of nonverbal communication.

Wood, Denis. *The Power of Maps*. New York: Guilford Press, 1992.
This well-documented study analyzes the symbolisms inherent in maps and discusses maps as conveyors of subtle as well as obvious messages.

Author and Title Index

This index is to authors and titles discussed in Chapter 6 and elsewhere in the body of the book. It does not include works cited in the Selected Annotated Bibliography or in the chapter notes.

Subject Index

African Americans, in library catalog, 112–113

Anthologies, as student projects, 50

Arabic names, 18–19

Archives, 43; locating, 96–98. *See also* Primary sources

Assessment of student work. *See* Evaluation of student work

Assignments, research, 49–57. *See also* Topics for student research

Assignments, structuring, 34–36

Assignments not requiring library research, 57–66

Assignments suitable for groups. *See* Group projects

Associations: directories of, 81–82; as topics for student research, 38–39

Atlases, 82–83

Autobiographies, fictional, as student projects, 65

Autobiographies: sources of, 84–87, 95; as student projects, 59

Bilingualism, 27

Biographies: sources of, 84–87; as topics for student research, 37–38

Brochures and leaflets, as student projects, 64–65

Case studies: as student projects, 52–53; use in classroom, 30

Chinese names, 19

Chronologies, 82–83

Classroom strategies and activities: for diversity, 21–30; guidelines for discussions, 72–73; to overcome resistance to diversity, 71–73

Content analysis of media, 61

Critical reading and viewing, 23, 51, 58

Critical thinking: as aid in curriculum development, 10; as basis for diversity in curriculum, 4

Curriculum. *See* Diversity in the curriculum; Syllabi

Curriculum revision, stages of, 2–3

Dialogues, as student projects, 53–54

Directories, 81–82

Diversity in the curriculum: models of, 2–3; overcoming student resistance to, 71–73; reasons for not including, 3–5; strategies for adding, 10–14; student resistance to, 69–70. *Specific disciplines cited in examples:* art, 57, 64; business, 53; economics, 64, 65; foreign languages, 62; government, 63, 64; history, 51, 52–53, 57,

ABOUT THE AUTHOR

MARILYN LUTZKER is Chief Librarian and Professor at the John Jay College of Criminal Justice. Her previous publications include *Criminal Justice Research in Libraries* with Eleanor Ferrall (1986) and *Research Projects for College Students: What to Write Across the Curriculum* (1988), both published by Greenwood Press.